T0332000

Deindustrialization, Distribution, and Development

Deindustrialization, Distribution, and Development

Structural Change in the Global South

Andy Sumner

OXFORD

UNIVERSITY PRESS

Great Clarendon Street, Oxford, OX2 6DP,
United Kingdom

Oxford University Press is a department of the University of Oxford.
It furthers the University's objective of excellence in research, scholarship,
and education by publishing worldwide. Oxford is a registered trade mark of
Oxford University Press in the UK and in certain other countries

First Edition published in 2021

Impression: 1

Published in the United States of America by Oxford University Press
198 Madison Avenue, New York, NY 10016, United States of America

British Library Cataloguing in Publication Data

Data available

Library of Congress Control Number: 2021936802

ISBN 978-0-19-885300-8

DOI: 10.1093/oso/9780198853008.001.0001

Printed and bound by
CPI Group (UK) Ltd, Croydon, CR0 4YY

The motivations of the investigator are numerous. The most fundamental, however, is confidence in one's own imagination—and knowledge of how to use it.

Celso Furtado (2009 [1998], p. 9).

Acknowledgements

I would like to thank the following: Luciano Ciravegna, Kathleen Craig, Salome Ecker, Andrew Fischer, Kyunghoon Kim, Pedro Paredes Llanos, Terry McKinley, Eduardo Ortiz-Juarez, Nicola Phillips, Enrique de la Rosa Ramos, Alfredo Saad-Filho, Diding Sakri, Lukas Schlogl, Ben Selwyn, Alberto Smith, Kunal Sen, and Arief Yusuf.

Contents

List of Figures

List of Tables

List of Abbreviations

CEPAL	Comisión Económica para América Latina y el Caribe [United Nations Economic Commission for Latin America and the Caribbean]
GATT	General Agreement on Tariffs and Trade
GDP	gross domestic product
GGDC	Groningen Growth and Development Centre
GNI	gross national income
GVC	global value chain
HIC	high-income country
IMF	International Monetary Fund
LIC	low-income country
LDC	least developed country
LMIC	lower middle-income country
MIC	middle-income country
ODA	official development assistance
OECD	Organisation for Economic Co-operation and Development
PPP	purchasing power parity
R&D	research and development
SME	small and medium-sized enterprises
SOE	state-owned enterprise
TFP	total factor productivity
TIVA	Trade in Value Added
TNC	transnational corporation
UMIC	upper middle-income country
UN	United Nations
UNCTAD	United Nations Conference on Trade and Development
UNDP	United Nations Development Programme
UNIDO	United Nations Industrial Development Organization
UNSD	United Nations Statistics Division
UNU-WIDER	United Nations University World Institute for Development Economics Research
US	United States
WTO	World Trade Organization

1

Introduction

1.1 The Myth

In *O Mito do Desenvolvimento Econômico* Celso Furtado (2020a [1974]) discussed the 'myth' of economic development.[1] The myth for Furtado was that *economic development*, as it has been practiced by the countries that led the Industrial Revolution, can be universalised' (p. 2) and as a result *'poor peoples* can one day enjoy the lifestyles of currently *rich peoples'* (p. 63, emphases as original). The purpose of this and any myth for Furtado was to 'function as lighthouses that illuminate the perceptual field...allowing...a clear vision of certain problems and to see nothing of others' (p. 1).

Furtado's 'myth' remains today the common discourse on the economic catch-up of poor peoples and poor countries (or in the case of the latter, what he refers to as peripheral or underdeveloped countries) with the rich(er) peoples and advanced industrial countries of the world (or core economies). Furtado argued that the superstructure of the world's capitalist economy— the International Monetary Fund (IMF) and the General Agreement on Tariffs and Trade (GATT, later the World Trade Organization (WTO))— would limit the universalizability of the advanced countries' industrial revolution. Periphery countries could progress, though economic growth may come without economic development he posited. As peripheral economies grew, he argued that national inequality would inevitably rise and consequentially, only the top five to ten per cent of the population of developing countries could ever achieve the living standards of developed countries. Furtado put it thus:

> [T]he predominant evolutionary tendency is to exclude nine people out of ten from the principal benefits of development, and if we observe the group of peripheral countries in particular, we realise that the tendency there is to exclude nineteen out of twenty. (p. 62)

[1] Furtado (2020a [1974]) was written as a response to the 'Limits to Growth' report of the Club of Rome and its dire predictions related to economic growth and planetary boundaries. The English translation cited here is of the abridged Portuguese version. See also Furtado (2020b).

Deindustrialization, Distribution, and Development: Structural Change in the Global South. Andy Sumner, Oxford University Press. © Andrew Sumner 2021. DOI: 10.1093/oso/9780198853008.003.0001

The ten per cent figure is based on a rough estimate that the income per capita of core countries is ten times that of peripheral countries (Furtado (2020a [1974], p. 59). Furtado wrote of this myth over forty years ago. Today in exchange rate terms, the average income of advanced countries (high-income countries (HICs) or OECD members) is indeed tenfold that of developing countries (low- and middle-income countries, LICs and MICs) or respectively approximately $5,000 versus $50,000 in GNI per capita (World Bank, 2020). And the average proportion of the population of a developing country in 2018 living at a level approximate to being non-poor in a richer nation is, as Furtado predicted, about 10 per cent (Furtado (2020a [1974, p. 59).[2]

Four decades after Furtado wrote of his myth, the book at hand argues that there is a new mirage of economic development that has strong resonance with Furtado's myth though with new, contemporary characteristics. The global capitalist superstructure that Furtado pointed to has been reshaped due to a set of inter-related, system-wide 'great transformations' leading to a structural evolution of the global economic system since the end of the Cold War. In contrast to Polanyi's (1957) 'great transformation'—the dis-embedding of the economy from society by processes of commodification—the set of inter-related transformations identified in this book relate to the changes in the global economy since the end of the Cold War that have led to a dis-embedding of what can be called 'deep' industrialization as per the advanced nations from the very idea of economic development in developing countries. Each of the four transformations which will be outlined shortly has an accompanying myth related to economic development. It is the juxtaposition of these myths that produces the *mirage* of economic development. Put another way, the four transformations of the global system, and the accompanying myths each transformation has generated, have reconfigured Furtado's myth in a new, more complex guise operating as a set of constraining parameters to the qualitative nature of, and quantitative extent of, economic development attainable by developing countries. Deep industrialization—like the industrialization of advanced countries—is evaporating as an idea and practice and is being replaced with a diminishing form—shallow and stunted—of economic development rather than one which is a genuine economic transformation.

This is diminishing development. It is diminished compared to a more substantive meaning of economic development—as taken in this book—that

---

[2] Even in PPP$ the GNI per capita of advanced countries is fivefold, respectively approximately $10,000 versus $50,000. See discussion in Chapter 2 on these matters, including new estimates.

encapsulates a genuinely transformative, emancipatory economic development in keeping with Furtado's (1965, pp. 39–40) own definition of economic development as 'a process of social change through which a growing number of human necessities, pre-existing or created through the change itself, are satisfied through a differentiation in the productive system generated by the introduction of technological innovation' (though later in life Furtado delegated defining development to the masses (see Loureiro et al., 2020, p. 39–40). In other words, substantial and sustained structural transformation as per Seers' (1963, pp. 81–3) codification of the 'special case' of advanced nations.

What then are the four great transformations of the global economy and their accompanying myths that have led to diminishing development? The first great transformation is the shift in most developing countries, due to economic growth, from aid-dependence to countries where traditional aid (official development assistance) is much less significant vis-à-vis the size of domestic resources. In short, some aspects of the superstructure of the 1970s when Furtado wrote of the myth—the IMF and World Bank—matter *less* today, as in most developing countries aid is less important. It remains to be seen if the COVID-19 pandemic and its aftermath will change this. Other aspects, notably the GATT, now the WTO remain, as does the dominance of transnational corporations (TNCs).[3] At the same time this has happened under a new mode of orchestration of global production which does not necessarily require the ownership of production by TNCs. Accompanying the undeniable economic growth that has been achieved in many developing countries, there is a shift of many people—living in absolute poverty at low poverty lines at least—to a burgeoning new precariat class (to use the term of Standing, 2011) living in a fuzzy zone between absolute poverty and security from future poverty. As noted above, the data concurs with Furtado's forecast that only the top decile of the population of developing countries is likely to achieve the standards of living of the non-poor in advanced countries, at least to date. Precarity is likely to remain prevalent for many years given a shift of employment towards informal services. The myth accompanying this first transformation—substantial economic growth and consequentially, the decline in importance of aid in many developing countries—is that growth has become easier, and thus that the process of economic development has become ahistorical, even easy. In reality, this book argues, 'late development' remains a crucial concept in understanding contemporary development.

---

[3] Furtado (2020a [1974], p. 70, n. 17) preferred to use 'large companies' as he argued every large company is international in the sense of operating in various countries, even if the capital is controlled by a nation state: 'the difference between "national" and "international" tends to secondary; what matters most is the relative clout of the company'.

A second great transformation is the empirically observable shift in many middle-income developing countries towards an era of stalled industrialization and the spectre of premature deindustrialization (a term first coined by the United Nations Conference on Trade and Development (UNCTAD) 2003: VII). This second transformation demonstrates the diminishing of development by the dis-embedding of industrialization from economic development. To be precise, developing countries' deindustrialization refers to the predicament whereby the relative size of manufacturing activity peaks, stagnates, and declines as a proportion of the total economy. The process commences prematurely in the sense—it is argued by Palma (2005, 2008) and Rodrik (2016) amongst others—that it may occur at much lower levels of income per capita and at lower peaks of manufacturing's share in employment and value-added than experienced by early industrializing nations. The myth accompanying this second transformation is that economic development has always been, or has become, sector-neutral. As we discuss in this book, manufacturing remains preferable to tertiary-led economic development in the sense of delivering substantial value-added *and* formal sector employment growth in developing countries.

A third great transformation has taken place in the global economy—noted briefly above—which is the emergence of a new organization of global production. That is an organization of production in global value chains (GVCs). In other words, a 'GVC world' has emerged, in which the global production process has shifted from generally nationally or regionally integrated production into internationally fragmented production (Phillips, 2017). Stages of the production process have become dispersed across various countries and are orchestrated rather than necessarily owned by TNCs. This shift has turned developing economies into peripheral suppliers to GVCs with the developed countries remaining home to most of the largest or lead TNCs in each chain. As a direct result, industrialization has been dis-embedded from economic development because the deep economic development of extensive domestic industry and attainment of advanced economic structures achieved by the advanced nations has been abandoned in favour of a diminished or shallow and stunted economic development of a relatively small number of globally competitive national companies slotting into GVCs. The myth accompanying this third transformation that this book challenges is thus: For developing countries, more and more integration into GVC-world will drive and sustain economic development—value-added and employment—in the long term to the level of the advanced countries.

A fourth great transformation is the shift from more equitable forms of economic growth to an immiserizing one. Growth is immiserizing in three senses in a GVC world: First, growth is accompanied by falling labour shares—to maintain international competitiveness in a GVC world—which is associated with rising national income inequality. Second, growth is immiserizing in the sense that the falling labour share manifests in weak employment growth in the modern sector. Third, growth is immiserizing in the sense that the main labour movement is from a higher wage, more equal and more formalized sector (with relatively better pay and conditions)—formal manufacturing—to less equal, informal manufacturing, or informal services. The myth accompanying this fourth transformation that this book challenges is thus: if developing countries integrate more and more into GVC world, the process will lead to broad-based economic development, not just progress for the top ten per cent or the high skilled part of the population.

The four great transformations have created the new mirage of economic development. This mirage is a consequence of the transformations and their accompanying myths that have led to the dis-embedding of industrialization from the actual idea as well as practice of economic development. The new mirage is—in keeping with Furtado—that most developing countries and poor peoples are on a journey towards some day catching up with advanced countries and rich peoples through the integration into global production. The reality is, as this book argues, that few, if any, developing countries beyond China will ever truly get anywhere close to catching up with the structural characteristics associated with advanced nations and the deep industrialization the advanced nations achieved, meaning the development of a range of industries rather than simply a few internationally competitive companies with a 'slot' in a GVC. The economic development achieved by advanced countries is the classic case of industrialization and the benchmark against which the late development of contemporary developing countries is to be compared to in this book. Furthermore, the book argues that the COVID-19 pandemic and aftermath will speed up the trends this book discusses. In fact, it is even possible the pandemic will act as a 'super-accelerator' as the processes of stalled industrialization and premature dein-dustrialization and tertiarization in developing countries become part of the new normal for developing countries post-pandemic (see for discussion, Baldwin, 2020a, 2020b).

This introductory chapter is structured as follows: Section 1.2 discusses the contribution of the book. Section 1.3 gives a brief history of development since the Cold War. Section 1.4 discusses the theses of the book. Section 1.5 covers the methodology and methods of the book. Section 1.6 reviews the existing literature in this area and the gap the book addresses. Section 1.7

outlines the structure of the book, chapter by chapter. Section 1.8 concludes the introduction.

1.2 This Book

This book builds upon previous work by the author on economic development, structural change, and income inequality (see Sumner, 2016, 2018). The core foci of the book at hand are the structural evolution of the global system through the four great transformations and their associated myths of economic development, the dis-embedding of industrialization from economic development, and the consequential processes of stalled industrialization and premature deindustrialization which are creating a new 'rust belt'. This term, rust belt, has been rarely associated with developing countries to date. In fact, it is commonly associated with deindustrialization in advanced countries and the US in particular. However, such a belt is threatening the middle-income developing world, starting from Brazil and other countries in Latin America, running down across South Africa, and then upwards to Malaysia, Indonesia, Thailand, and the Philippines in South East Asia. Hence, a new rust belt is beginning to encircle the manufacturing of the developing world. Put simply, these trends signal the end of the old school kind of *speedster* economic development which was manufacturing-led and has been most evident in East Asia and China and which generated value-added and substantive employment predicated on the manufacturing sector.

Manufacturing expansion in developing countries is key to reducing both components of global inequality: within and between countries inequality. The link between manufacturing and global inequality is thus: the expansion of manufacturing value-added fuels faster economic growth and hence has the power to reduce between-country inequality. At the same time, manufacturing also has more potential than any other sector to expand wage employment opportunities and thus to decrease the within-country component of global inequality.

The emergence of the new rust belt means that global inequality is likely to 'boomerang' in the next decade or so. In short, the declining trend of global inequality from around the mid-2000s to the present—largely driven by a fall in the between-country component of global inequality—is likely to be temporary. This is due to the fact that the catch-up process will slow down as MICs shift from industrialization to deindustrialization. Additionally, national inequality—the within-country component of global inequality—is likely to increase as economic growth generates fewer better-paid manufacturing jobs and workers move into the low-wage, informal services sector work.

To understand these changes late development is an important concept: when countries try to industrialize, the process of structural change and the context, nature, and rules are shaped by those who industrialized prior. Late development implicitly recognizes the structural disadvantage late developers face as a result of history; and captures the importance to late developers of patterns of global accumulation and their interaction with national accumulation and social structures. Late development thus provides the point of departure in this book for building a production-based theory of global inequality. This book thus emphasizes the renewed relevance of late development to understanding contemporary economic development and the dominance of the global capitalist economy in the late economic development of developing countries. It is argued that late development is particularly crucial to comprehend the processes of stalled industrialization, premature deindustrialization, and tertiarization in developing countries.

In the following section a brief history of late development since 1990 is provided in order to set the scene for the main theses of the book which are outlined in the section that follows after.

1.3   A Brief History of Late Development since 1990

Since the end of the Cold War, global income inequality overall has fallen. This has been driven by a fall in the between-country component of global inequality in particular. At the same time, the within-country component of global inequality has risen in some countries such as China and Indonesia while falling in others, notably in Latin America.

Some developing economies have been catching up to some extent, although even those developing countries are a long way from OECD countries in terms of GDP per capita, let alone the economic structure associated with advanced countries. Moreover, the decline in global inequality is almost entirely attributable to the economic development of China. In short, any claims of a 'great convergence' are largely due to one country, albeit one that comprises a fifth of the world's population. Other developing economies beyond China have experienced economic growth, especially so during the commodity boom years of the 2000s, which has hidden to some extent the less benign processes of stalled industrialization, deindustrialization, and tertiarization.

The economic development model promoted since the Cold War by international agencies (e.g. UNCTAD, 2013; UNIDO, 2018; World Bank, 2019b) albeit with caveats has been that developing countries should expand their manufacturing output—as manufacturing provides a host of social and economic benefits—through assimilation into global production networks and specifically, into the GVCs that form those networks, whereby the different stages of the production process are dispersed across different countries and, in some cases, *many* different countries.

Without a doubt, it is true that export-led manufacturing has been a significant catalyst for economic development and job creation in many countries in the past, notably East Asia from the 1970s to the early-to-mid-1990s (see discussion of Southeast Asia in Sumner, 2018). Furthermore, in middle-income developing countries, productivity is generally higher in the formal manufacturing sector—or what Furtado called the 'nucleus' sector and Lewis (1954) referred to as the 'modern' sector in which modern technology is utilized; and which sits in contrast to what Furtado called the 'backward' or Lewis the 'traditional' sector, which is often taken to mean low-productivity subsistence agriculture. Consequently, industrialization has historically brought about impressive economic growth opportunities for developing countries through the expansion of the modern manufacturing sector. In fact, the modern manufacturing sector has been considered 'special' in terms of fostering broad-based economic development since at least post-WWII development economics (see, for example, Lewis, 1954, 1979; Kaldor, 1957, 1966, 1967); and more broadly what can be called the classical school of economic development.

Empirical support for the manufacturing and economic growth link is abundant (see, for example, Duarte and Restuccia, 2010; Herrendorf et al., 2014; McMillan et al., 2014). Developing countries that have experienced industrialization to date have reaped those social and economic benefits from the advancement of the sector. However, the nature of structural transformation—namely industrialization—has changed post-1990 and diminished in meaning from a 'deep' industrialization of building entire major industries to a 'shallow' industrialization of slotting into specific points of global production as a result of the fragmentation of global production into GVCs. In short, industrialization has come to be sought *without* the building of entire domestic industries and instead as a diminished form of industrialization based on GVC participation via domestic suppliers, often just a few internationally competitive domestic companies.

To optimists (e.g. Baldwin, 2016), this is good news, as in the past a country had to master the production of a whole manufactured product in order to begin exporting it. GVCs, it is argued, make industrialization easier since GVCs allow countries to specialize in manufacturing activities or tasks that can readily be developed within the domestic economy and it is no longer necessary to develop entire industries. Developing countries can specialize in particular stages of, or inputs into, global production and simply slot into GVCs where they have, or can develop, domestic supplier firms who are internationally competitive in costs, standards, and logistics.

The less optimistic perspective for developing countries is well illustrated in Shih's (1996), misleadingly named for developing countries, 'smile curve'. The smile curve is represented in a graph format with the vertical axis as value-added and the horizontal axis showing the sequence of activities in the value chain from beginning (i.e. design) to end (i.e. marketing). Shih (1996) argued, using the personal computer industry as an example, that the higher-value-added activities take place at the beginning and at the end of the value chain. In contrast, the actual assembly of the computer in the middle of the value chain is a relatively lower-value-added activity.[4] Much developing country activity focuses on assembly tasks in the *middle* of GVCs and adds less value than activities as the beginning and end stages of GVCs (Mudambi, 2008; Shin et al., 2012).

There are also bigger questions regarding the relationship between the creation and distribution of value across the chain between developing and developed countries, the extent to which developing countries are 'locked' in lower-value-added parts of GVCs, and what developing countries can do in terms of 'upgrading'. Upgrading in GVCs—for example, from assembly to product design or marketing—is far from easy (Gereffi, 1999). Higher-value-added activities remain dominated by lead TNCs in each value chain and such activities are likely to be situated in OECD countries. Thus, GVC participation may help developing countries initially with shallow industrialization through some growth in productivity and exports, but long-term or deep economic development may be *stunted*, especially so if technology reduces the demand for low-skilled labour abundant in developing countries. Furthermore, while GVC participation may benefit a small group of firms who have the capabilities to enter global markets, there is only limited job creation or a bias towards higher-skilled or non-routine labour. In sum, the benefits from GVC participation are non-linear and accrue at lower income

---

[4] Furthermore, there is evidence that smile curves are deepening, which would entail even lower relative value-added activities in the assembly stage vis-à-vis the beginning or end of the GVC. For example, Ye et al. (2015) find, using World Input-Output Database (WIOD) data for 1995–2011, evidence that 'smile curves' have been deepening and widening over time. They focus on Chinese and Mexican electrical products and German and Japanese auto value chains.

levels but then diminish or may even turn negative for employment or value-added at productivity levels associated with middle-income developing countries.

The emergence of this GVC world has coincided with an unexpected phenomenon in the developing world in recent years. Many middle-income developing countries are witnessing the emergence of the new middle-income rust belt. These countries are undergoing a process of stalled industrialization or even premature deindustrialization accompanied by tertiarization. In other words, the social and economic benefits that manufacturing usually offers are being exhausted earlier than has historically been the case for other countries. The manufacturing share of employment and value-added in the modern—i.e. GVC-integrated—manufacturing sector has peaked in many middle-income developing countries at a lower level than had been the case for early industrializers and/or at lower levels of income per capita.

What is *surprising* is that stalled industrialization, premature deindustrialization, and tertiarization have been occurring in the very same MICs heavily embedded within GVCs. These contemporary patterns of late economic development—stalled industrialization, deindustrialization, and tertiarization—occurring in many middle-income developing countries are now well documented (see, for example, Amirapu and Subramanian, 2015; Dasgupta and Singh, 2006; Felipe et al., 2014; Frenkel and Rapetti, 2012; Herrendorf et al., 2013; Palma, 2005, 2008; Pieper, 2000; Rodrik, 2016; Szirmai and Verspagen, 2011; Tregenna, 2009, 2014).

What is more startling to note is that there is no *overall* global deindustrialization in terms of the share of manufacturing of the entire global economy. This seems paradoxical given the experiences of many MICs. Felipe and Mehta (2016) show empirically that the manufacturing shares of both output and employment have remained surprisingly stable at global levels since the 1970s, at least up to 2010. In corroboration of the finding that there is no deindustrialization of manufacturing at a global level at least to 2010, Haraguchi et al. (2017) provide evidence showing that, on average, there are constant shares of manufacturing in developing countries alongside a trend towards the concentration of manufacturing in fewer developing countries, especially in China. In sum, overall manufacturing shares are globally steady. However, there are tectonic shifts have taken place in terms of where manufacturing is performed, leading to deindustrialization in some middle-income developing countries whilst there is—paradoxically—no overall global deindustrialization. Felipe and Mehta (2016) also show that large within-country manufacturing productivity growth was counterbalanced by a massive movement of manufacturing employment to populous, lower-productivity economies. Put simply, manufacturing jobs have been spread thinner and thinner across more and more countries, hence it has become harder to sustain high levels of manufacturing employment in individual countries. Furthermore, Felipe et al. (2014, 2018) worryingly note that the achievement of high-income status for a country depends on it reaching a certain level of peak manufacturing employment (18 to 20 per cent), which few if any developing countries today are likely to attain. This raises questions as to whether today's MICs will become HICs.

1.4   The Theses of the Book

There have been a number of studies focusing on these processes of stalled industrialization and deindustrialization. However, these studies have not sought to situate the emergence of deindustrialization as well as the persistence of global inequality within a GVC-dominated global economy. This is why this book brings together these three hitherto unconnected phenomena—stalled industrialization and premature deindustrialization, global inequality, and the emergence of a GVC world.

The first thesis of this book is as follows: after the Cold War, the economies of the developing world accelerated liberalization, encouraged or pushed by the IMF and World Bank in the hubris of the triumph of capitalism. This liberalization, together with changes in technology and transportation, enabled a restructuring of global production that suited the interests of international capital in the form of TNCs. It allowed TNCs to fragment the production of a single final product across many countries and to locate production based on cost and logistics. Thereby, a GVC world was created. The mantra of international organizations was, and remains, that developing countries no longer need to develop entire domestic industries but should just choose an 'access point' to a specific GVC, and hence become part of GVC world as suppliers, using that to pursue economic development and stimulate job creation.

Secondly, this book argues that since the Cold War, there has been much economic growth in most developing countries, which has generated a new bifurcation within what was the developing world. This bifurcation has split the formerly homogenous group into zero-growth developing countries and 'moving' developing countries. The former refers to a small set of developing countries which remain very poor and heavily aid-dependent. The latter are a large set of much of the developing world where aid is far less significant vis-à-vis domestic resources. The former have barely begun the pathway to industrialization. The latter have achieved much to date and built manufacturing which has powered economic development in terms of job creation and some catch-up with developed countries. Stalled industrialization and premature deindustrialization now threaten these gains. Furthermore, growth has produced two new 'middles', the first of which refers to the moving countries or new MICs themselves. The second middle describes the many people in MICs whose incomes have risen above absolute poverty. However, the poverty lines they have exceeded are low and their new incomes are not too far above absolute poverty. Hence, these people are not secure from the risk of future poverty induced by an economic slow-down that stalled industrialization and deindustrialization are associated with.

Third, although there has not been a global deindustrialization, the manufacturing that has taken place in the developing world has been spread over more and more countries. As a consequence, value-added and jobs are spread more thinly. This constrains the benefits of manufacturing levels that might be achieved and weakens growth prospects because individual countries are unable to capture enough of global production to achieve a deep(er) industrialization. In other words, developing countries find themselves in a new kind of middle-income or 'rust belt bind' of stalled industrialization or outright deindustrialization, as more and more developing countries compete over the same value chains and entry points.

Finally, this book argues that stalled industrialization or deindustrialization-led growth has exacerbated inequality both between and within countries. Global inequality between countries has been intensified because economic growth during stalled industrialization or deindustrialization has been slower than manufacturing-led growth has historically been. On the other hand, deindustrialization-led growth has exacerbated inequality within countries because workers have moved from the modern—GVC-integrated—manufacturing sector, which has higher average wages, a more equal distribution, and is likely to be a relatively more unionized sector, to an expanding informal sector, which is less equal and has lower average wages. This development has been further intensified by the fact that many workers have moved to informal services in particular, and into low-wage, precarious, and low-productivity work.

What will be the impact of the COVID-19 pandemic on the theses of this book? The pandemic is likely to accelerate the trends this book outlines, possibly dramatically so. This is because of the disruptive impact of COVID-19 on global manufacturing production itself and the fact that as one region recovers, GVCs may be disrupted further due to the pandemic and its aftermath. The lockdowns put in place to varying degrees including temporary factory closures will mean various global macro-economic shocks and national economic shocks to production. Thus, the impact of the pandemic will likely be an accelerator of the processes of stalled industrialization and deindustrialization in output in developing countries outlined in this book.

In that vein, Baldwin (2020a) argues that the COVID-19 pandemic will have an impact via three channels. First, a supply disruption on production as the pandemic originated in the world's 'manufacturing heartland' in East Asia and spread to the US and Germany, who are also central to global production networks. Second, a contagion effect whereby even the manufacturing in less impacted countries will find it harder or costlier to source industrial imported inputs. Third, a demand disruption due to recessions, delayed purchasing by consumers, and delayed investment by firms.

Furthermore, the pandemic and its aftermath could impact the processes of stalled industrialization and deindustrialization via changes in employment. Tertiarization may become more rapid as service jobs in OECD countries move from offices to remote working in OECD countries and then to digitally 'tele-migrating' service sector workers in developing countries (Baldwin, 2020b). As a result of COVID-19 many firms have invested heavily in digital working, meaning an acceleration of service jobs relocation to developing countries, as remote working is far more plausible. In sum, the pandemic could lead to an acceleration of the trends outlined in this book.

1.5 Methodology and Methods

The methodological approach utilized in this book follows the tradition of the early pioneers of development economics, notably Celso Furtado, and also W. Arthur Lewis, Nicholas Kaldor, and Simon Kuznets. The approach is one of Kaldorian theory building based on stylized facts—historical reflections or what Keynes called 'vigilant observation'—based on the quantitative study of how developing countries experience the process of economic development and structural transformation. Kaldor (1961, pp. 177–8) put it thus:

> We all agree that the basic requirement of any model is that it should be capable of explaining the characteristic features of the economic process as we find them in reality. It is no good starting off a model with the kind of abstraction which initially excludes the influence of forces which are mainly responsible for the behaviour of the economic variables under investigation...Any theory must necessarily be based on abstractions; but the type of abstraction chosen cannot

be decided in a vacuum...Hence the theorist, in choosing a particular theoretical approach, ought to start off with a summary of the facts which he regards as relevant to his problem. Since facts, as recorded by statisticians, are always subject to numerous snags and qualifications, and for that reason are incapable of being accurately summarized, the theorist, in my view, should be free to start with a 'stylized' view of the facts – i.e. concentrate on broad tendencies, ignoring individual detail, and proceed on the 'as if' method, i.e. construct a hypothesis that could account for these 'stylized' facts.

In keeping with Kaldor's approach, this book builds theory chapter by chapter based on stylized facts. Precisely because statistics are 'always subject to numerous snags and qualifications' to echo Kaldor above, this book does not pursue advanced statistical techniques. Rather, the book makes Keynesian 'vigilant observations' through description and analysis of longer-term trends, patterns, and regularities, or the kind of quantitative economic history that is associated with Furtado, Kuznets, and Lewis too. In short, the book takes Selwyn's (2011) dialectical approach to development, that is the use of data analysis methods to investigate historical trends and regularities. This way, theory is built that includes the interaction of global economic structures with systems of national capital accumulation:

A dialectical approach implies a theory of a dynamic, transformative system (capitalism), combined with a conception of how the unequal units of the system are internally constituted and externally connected...This approach...strives to account for (1) the evolving world system, (2) the timing of backward economies' catch-up attempts and (3) how domestic social structures interact with international forces to influence a country's developmental trajectory

(Selwyn, 2011, p. 425).

Empirically, the book makes extensive use of the Groningen Growth and Development Centre (GGDC) 10-Sector Database, 2015 version (see Timmer et al., 2015 for discussion). The GGDC 10-Sector Database allows for analysis of changes in employment, productivity, and value-added at a sectoral level for ten sectors. In principle, the GGDC 10-Sector database covers both formal and informal manufacturing. This is a reasonable assumption to make for employment data, though the precise extent to which it is the case for value-added data depends on national sources (Diao et al., 2017, pp. 4–6). Further, we make use of two UN datasets. First, the UNIDO IND-STAT2, 2018 version, which covers only formal (or 'modern' in Lewisian terms) manufacturing with data on employment and value-added shares by 20 subsectors (see UNIDO, 2019). Second, the UNSD National Accounts Main Aggregates Database, 2018 version (see UNSD, 2018).[5]

Finally, we make use of two other datasets: one from Pahl and Timmer (2020) in discussion of the outcomes of GVC-participation (based in part on the UNIDO IND-STAT2 dataset above) and one from Baymul and Sen (2020) (which itself is based on the GGDC 10-Sector database above and a standardization version of the UNU-WIDER World Income Inequality Database).

Two broad issues should be highlighted at the outset. As Fischer (2011, 2014) notes—resonating with the Kaldor quote earlier—one important limitation of the available data is whether productivity can be accurately measured in a complex economy. Measuring productivity relies on value-added account data, but such data is a combination of output and prices/wages. Therefore, most measurements for productivity show price or wage differentials instead of actual effort, output, or skill. This is an even bigger problem in the service sector, as comparability of services is more problematic because there are no physical goods that can be compared.

Fischer (2014) also notes another problem, namely that Southern subsidiaries of TNCs might look less productive than they actually are. This might be the case because TNCs—who dominate production and coordinate GVCs—conduct practices such as transfer pricing and the transferring of profits from Southern subsidiaries to Northern headquarters (for example, low-interest loans from subsidiary to parent company). These are clearly important issues that, although not easily resolved, should be kept in mind as the reader navigates the discussion of this book.

1.6 The Existing Literature

Many seminal studies exist which detail 'good' and 'bad' deindustrialization in OECD countries. The former, 'good' deindustrialization, generally entails new employment to absorb laid-off manufacturing workers in tertiary sectors (see Alderson, 1999; Bacon and Eltis, 1976; Bazen and Thirlwall, 1986, 1989, 1992; Bluestone and Harrison, 1982; Cairncross, 1979; Fontagné and Harrison, 2017; De Groot, 2000; Kucera and Milberg, 2003; Linkon, 2018; Rowthorn and Ramaswamy, 1997; Saeger, 1997; Thirlwall, 1982; Wren, 2013).

---

[5] In contrast, the World Bank's World Development Indicators (WDI) dataset provides data on 140 developing countries (with gaps) but only three sectors (agriculture, industry, and services). Furthermore, manufacturing employment is not disaggregated by industry.

There is also a set of influential papers which discuss the inverted-U curve of the manufacturing share of employment in OECD countries as the defining pattern of deindustrialization (e.g. Rowthorn and Wells, 1987; Rowthorn and Coutts, 2004; Rowthorn and Ramaswamy, 1997; Singh, 1977, 1987).

Caution is needed when using these studies of OECD countries as a template for middle-income developing countries because the effects of deindustrialization may be different in the contemporary developing world. One reason for differences is that the process of deindustrialization can happen at lower levels of per capita income and lower 'peak manufacturing' (in terms of value-added and employment shares). Furthermore, contemporary deindustrialization occurs at a different point in history, as global production is now highly fragmented into GVCs.

Moreover, in middle-income developing countries, the economic strategies and welfare regime mechanisms mitigating the impact of deindustrialization—ranging from unemployment benefits and pensions to access to health and retraining programmes—are weaker and cover a lower share of the population than in advanced economies. It is also unlikely that middle-income developing countries can respond to deindustrialization by mimicking advanced economies; that is, focusing on downstream, higher-value activities (e.g. marketing and the development of creative content) or on upstream activities linked to science and technology. In downstream activities, advanced economies benefit from having consumers with higher incomes, a freer civil society, world class universities in the creative industries and sciences, and well-established firms that lead GVCs. All of these yield positive reputational effects, e.g. 'made in France' for leather products or 'made in Germany' for automotive products. In upstream, science-intensive activities (e.g. new materials, pharmacological research, and aerospace), middle-income developing countries compete with advanced economies who are worried about losing their dominance, and simultaneously with countries that challenge Western dominance such as China. Many OECD countries—e.g. France, Germany—as well as China heavily subsidize activities in order to either keep or capture the higher-value-added GVC access points.

Although much can be drawn from the research on OECD countries, caution is needed because the effects of deindustrialization are likely to be different in developing countries. The policy implications that are promoted (e.g. raising education levels and freer movement of labour) are often abstract and not sufficient in the current context of a world where industrial production is dominated by fragmented chains of production across numerous countries. Contemporary policy recommendations pay little attention to or make limited links with the structural global forces that will shape the future patterns of structural transformation. Available studies also say little on the state's role in supporting new sources of economic growth and job growth, and in managing a country's position in a GVC world.

In sum, the study of deindustrialization in developing countries in a GVC world and its consequences for between- and within-country inequality has received insufficient attention to date, with no recent monograph the author is aware of. There is a set of relevant cross-country papers noted previously (such as Palma, 2005, 2008; Rodrik, 2016) as well as single-country studies (e.g. for Malaysia, see Henderson and Phillips, 2007; Rasiah, 2011; Tan, 2014; for Indonesia, see Manning and Purnagunawan, 2017; for Mexico, see Cruz, 2014; for Chile, see Gwynne, 1986; for Pakistan, see Hamid and Khan, 2015; and for Brazil, see Jenkins, 2015b and Cypher, 2015). Few of these studies have, however, analysed the issues with reference to late economic development in a GVC world or in terms of global inequality.

1.7 The Structure of the Book

This book is structured as follows: Chapter 2 sets the scene in a panoramic discussion of changes in the developing world, in particular the economic growth since the 1990s. In doing so, the chapter focuses on the first great transformation outlined. It is argued that there is a new polarization in the developing world and that two new precarious 'middles'—one of countries and one of people—that have emerged since the end of the Cold War. Both are threatened by stalled industrialization and the spectre of deindustrialization. The chapter discusses the related myth emerging from this first transformation—that economic development is ahistorical. The chapter focuses on why late development remains a crucial concept in understanding contemporary development.

Chapter 3 then concentrates on the patterns of contemporary economic development and structural change. The chapter focuses on the second great transformation outlined. Specifically, it examines the evolution of late economic development towards stalled industrialization, deindustrialization, and tertiarization. The empirical basis of these patterns is explored anew. Furthermore, the myth accompanying this transformation—that economic development is sector-neutral—is discussed. Additionally, the extent to which patterns of late economic development—stalled industrialization, deindustrialization, and tertiarization—matter is considered. It is argued that (modern) manufacturing remains preferable to tertiary-led economic development.

Chapter 4 is concerned with the impact of deindustrialization on inequality between countries and the catch-up (or otherwise) of developing countries to date and in the years ahead. The chapter focuses on the third great transformation outlined, specifically the fragmentation of global production. This chapter discusses the debate on the impacts of changes in global production on middle-income developing countries and assesses the empirical evidence. The myth accompanying the third transformation—that if developing countries integrate more and more into GVC world, the process will drive and sustain economic development to the level of the advanced countries—is the subject of discussion in this chapter. Theory is developed to explain the connection between the emergence of a GVC world, deindustrialization, and economic growth in the developing world.

Chapter 5 addresses the within-country component of global inequality and the impact of deindustrialization on national income inequality. The chapter focuses on the fourth great transformation outlined, specifically the shift to a form of immiserizing growth. This chapter revisits Kuznets' seminal work and asks what trend might be expected for national inequality during deindustrialization. The chapter makes estimates of the empirical evidence on deindustrialization, tertiarization, and national income inequality in developing countries. The accompanying myth—that if developing countries integrate more and more into GVC world, the process will lead to broad-based economic development—is critiqued. A theoretical exposition to explain the connection between deindustrialization, tertiarization, and rising national income inequality in the developing world is given.

Finally, the concluding chapter summarizes the book's content and restates the main arguments of the book. There is discussion of the future prospects for developing countries and the 'tertiary trilemma' they face, specifically: Should middle-income developing countries pursue higher-value-added services-led growth which is unequalizing and has weaker employment growth? Or should they rather seek lower-value-added services-led growth which has higher employment growth? Or should they instead pursue the shrinkage of services and subsidize re-industrialization-led growth?

1.8 Conclusion

This book is about stalled industrialization, the spectre of premature deindustrialization, and tertiarization in the developing world. It discusses development since the 1960s/1970s and particularly since the 1990s. Four great transformations framing the evolution of the global system are presented, followed by a set of accompanying myths of economic development. The book culminates in the challenge that developing countries face in the 'tertiary trilemma' and the pursuit of national and equitable economic development in the years ahead.

It is argued throughout the book that the standard strategy of economic development promoted by international organizations since the Cold War, namely, the integration into global production, has engendered stalled industrialization, premature deindustrialization, and tertiarization. Furthermore, it is maintained that these effects will hinder the future catch-up of developing countries with developed nations. It is argued that these effects will exacerbate national income inequality and leave developing countries with a set of suboptimal choices that push them away from the speedster China model of manufacturing-led economic development towards the slower model of services-led economic development. This has consequences for inequality, employment, and economic growth if industrialization becomes permanently dis-embedded from economic development.

2

The Two New Middles

Bifurcation and Precarity in Late Economic Development

2.1 Introduction

This chapter is about the first great transformation. This transformation is the shift of most developing countries, due to economic growth, towards independence from aid. This applies to most, but not all, developing countries: economic growth has entailed a bifurcation of the developing world since the 1960s, and in particular since the 1990s. Although growth has waned since the mid-2000s, the increases over the longer period are significant. The myth accompanying this transformation—the declining importance of aid in many developing countries due to substantial economic growth—is that economic development is ahistorical. This chapter instead argues that late development remains a crucial concept in understanding contemporary development. The chapter thus situates the forthcoming discussion of stalled industrialization and the spectre of deindustrialization—the developing world's new 'rust belt'—within this broader panorama of contemporary development.

The bifurcation is evident between *and* within developing countries. Consequently, two new 'middles' have emerged. The first middle refers to countries: specifically, to the expansion of middle-income countries (MICs) due to economic growth and thus to a shift from a situation where traditional aid is important to most developing countries to a situation where traditional aid is of relatively insignificance compared to the size of domestic resources in most developing countries. The second new middle accompanying new MICs is a middle that comprises people. These people form a new 'middle' or a precariat class that, by certain standards, is living above day-to-day absolute poverty but who are not sufficiently far from poverty as to be secure from the risk of poverty in the future. The secure part of the population or the population living at or above non-poor Western standards is typically only the top 10 per cent or less, as Furtado (2020 [1974]) foresaw. In fact, an economic growth slow-down or weaker employment growth in the formal manufacturing sector, which stalled industrialization or deindustrialization

Deindustrialization, Distribution, and Development: Structural Change in the Global South. Andy Sumner, Oxford University Press.
© Andrew Sumner 2021. DOI: 10.1093/oso/9780198853008.003.0002

are likely to engender, may well mean that the new middle-income countries face economic stagnation. Similarly, for the new middle or precariat class, absolute poverty is not that far away if employment opportunities evaporate (or if there is a prolonged instability due to the COVID-19 pandemic and the aftermath).

This chapter thus argues that the developing world has fundamentally changed since the end of the 1960s and in particular since the 1990s, albeit in a more precarious way than it may seem at first. The chapter culminates in the critique of the myth that economic development is ahistorical and in a discussion of the foundational concept of 'late development'. In doing so we draw from a long line of scholars. Gerschenkron (1962) is typically credited with coining the term 'late industrialization' while Hirschman (1968, 1971) introduced the term 'late-late industrialization' though many others were using the concept including Furtado, Lewis, Kaldor, Kuznets, and other Structuralist thinkers (e.g. Prebisch, 1950; Singer, 1950; Myrdal, 1957a, 1957b, 1968, 1970; Sunkel, 1963; 1966, 1972, 1989, 1993) as well as those writing in the dependency school (e.g. Cardoso and Faletto, 1979; Dos Santos, 1970; Frank, 1966, 1972). Indeed, the idea is evident in much early theorizing in development economics even if it is not always explicitly labelled as 'late development' and more recently in the developmental state literature.[1]

Late development can be framed using Gerschenkron (1962) who argued that only the UK was an example of 'early' industrialization, meaning relatively uninfluenced by the global economy. All other countries were 'late' industrializers. Gerschenkron posited that each country that industrializes, changes the structure of the global economy as well as the country's own economic structures. The concept of late development is though not just about timing of industrialization. The concept is predicated on the sense that late industrializers face structural constraints.

In this chapter, the primary thesis is as follows: Substantial economic growth since the end of the 1960s, especially since 1990 and up to the mid-2000s when growth rates started to wane, has generated a new polarization or bifurcation within the developing world between a small group of very poor countries which remain highly aid-dependent and a large group of developing countries where aid is much less important. The former has

---

[1] As a consequence of late development, many scholars have highlighted the central role of the state in (late) economic development. For example, Lewis (1954) argued that only the state had the power to mobilize the capital and finance necessary. In a similar vein, Rosenstein-Rodan (1943) and Nurkse (1953) argued that the private sector would be unwilling to accept the risk. This crucial role of the state is central to the developmental state literature itself (e.g. Amsden, 1989, 2001; Chang, 1994, 2002; Johnson, 1982; Wade, 1990, 2014).

barely begun on the pathway to industrialization. Many of the latter have achieved much to date and built manufacturing which has powered economic development in terms of job creation and has led to some catch-up with developed countries. However, these gains are under threat not only from the economic instability due to the COVID-19 pandemic but—as this book will discuss—from the structural processes of stalled industrialization and the spectre of deindustrialization. In short, differing economic growth has produced bifurcation between and within developing countries and two new 'middles'. Specifically, a new middle of countries which are now middle-income according to average per capita income, although they face weakening growth prospects ahead due to stalled industrialization and deindustrialization. Secondly, a 'middle' of people, lifted above absolute poverty, at least when measured at low poverty lines, but who are not sufficiently far above as to be certain of not falling back into poverty. Indeed, an economic slowdown due to stalled industrialization is likely to push people back into poverty. In other words, they are living a life that is not far from absolute poverty and face the risk of falling back into absolute poverty if a reasonable rate of economic growth is not maintained for the foreseeable future, something that stalled industrialization and deindustrialization imply.

This chapter is structured as follows: Section 2.2 discusses the bifurcation of the developing world since the 1990s in particular. Section 2.3 then discusses the two new middles: specifically, the world's two new precarious middles of countries and people. Section 2.4 argues that the myth accompanying the first transformation—that substantial economic growth and the lesser importance of aid mean that economic development is ahistorical—is flawed; and that the concept of late development provides a point of departure for theory to explain the persistence and reproduction of global inequality. Section 2.5 concludes.

2.2 Convergence, Divergence, and Bifurcation

There has been much economic growth across most of the developing world since the end of the Cold War. This is good news although it has generated a new polarization within the developing world. In the 1960s, 1970s, and even towards the end of the 1980s, an argument, albeit contentious, could be made that the developing world was more homogenous. Now, the developing world is certainly not homogenous. Many developing countries would have once fallen into the characterization of being heavily aid-dependent. Fast forward to today and many are not. Rather, there is a new binary within the developing world between very poor, aid-dependent developing countries and developing countries where aid is of less importance due to the growth of domestic resources. Before we go further, it is worth pausing and noting that the changes identified in this chapter should not be read as absolutes. Rather, they are generalizable tendencies with exceptions.[2]

What actually changed? First, it is undeniable that there have been notable rises in mean gross domestic product (GDP) per person (and mean consumption per person) in most developing countries since the end of the Cold War. If one takes an arbitrary cut-off (see Table 2.1), there is a small set of less than 30 developing countries (with populations of 1 million or more) that remain very poor in the sense of very low or no economic growth since the end of the Cold War. This set of countries is home to less than one in ten of the population of the developing world. Most, but not all, of the slow-growth countries are low-income countries (LICs). In contrast, most of the developing world's population lives in countries that have grown substantially since 1990. This multi-speed world generates a binary between a group of countries that are likely to be poor for some time to come (possibly a very long time) and a larger set of developing countries which have been growing substantially into middle-income countries in average per capita terms, although they face the spectre of stalled industrialization and premature deindustrialization. It is important to remember, however, that the income gap between most developing countries and the developed countries is still enormous. Thus, there is a long way to go for all developing countries to catch up with the income per capita levels of OECD countries, let alone the structural characteristics of the advanced nations.

There is a related new binary as a result of variation in experience of economic growth within the developing world. The new binary is between highly aid-dependent developing countries and developing countries where 'traditional' official development assistance (ODA) is, or in the foreseeable future will be, less relevant vis-à-vis domestic resources.[3] If we take an arbitrary measure of ODA as five per cent or more of gross national income (GNI), less than 30 developing countries (with populations of 1 million or more) remain highly dependent on ODA (see Table 2.1). In these countries, the dominance of aid is likely to be evident across economic and social development as well as in governance. These countries are again home to about one in ten of the population living in developing countries. In contrast, almost 90 per cent of the population of the developing world lives in

[2] This chapter draws from ideas in Sumner (2019) and Edward and Sumner (2018, 2019).
[3] Early signs of the aid binary were identified in Maxwell (2006).

Table 2.1 Characteristics of developing countries by growth history (1990–2018) and ODA/GNI (2018)

	Number of countries	Percentage of developing world population (2018)
GDP per capita, PPP (constant 2011 international $), average annual growth, 1990–2018		
<1% per capita/year	28	9.2%
1–2% per capita/year	27	18.7%
>2% per capita/year	53	71.3%
No data	3	0.9%
Net ODA received as % of GNI, 2018		
<5%	73	86.9%
5–10%	15	6.0%
>10%	14	2.8%
No data	9	4.4%

Notes: Includes 111 developing countries with populations above 1 million people in 2018. No GDP per capita, PPP (constant 2011 international $) data available for DPR Korea, Somalia, and Syria. No net ODA received as percentage of GNI data available for Bulgaria, Cuba, DPR Korea, Romania, Russia, Somalia, South Sudan, Syria, and Venezuela.

Source: World Bank (2020).

countries where aid is less significant. There is—not surprisingly—some considerable overlap between these groups of slow-growth and aid-dependent countries.

In sum, substantial economic growth across much of the developing world is undeniable. It is not surprising that this has stimulated a 'sunshine' narrative, meaning an optimistic take on falling global inequality. This, however, has been oversold in the sense that the fall in global inequality is not evident in survey-based data if China is excluded. Furthermore, the fall in the between-country component of global inequality is not evident in estimates based on national accounts once China and India are excluded. We discuss this next.

What exactly has happened to global inequality since the Cold War? Figure 2.1 shows global inequality in two manifestations. The manifestations are firstly, global inequality as population-weighted inequality between countries' mean incomes and secondly, global inequality as population-weighted aggregated national or within-country inequality. Estimates here are from Edward and Sumner (2018) and are based on household survey data. They do not include adjustments for top income data on the basis that, as innovative as the endeavour to include such data may be, only 24 developing countries have these data readily available.[4]

---

[4] To date, Anand and Segal (2017) are the only scholars to make use of the full set of surveys and tax data available from the *World Inequality Database* which has data on 24 developing countries (see also

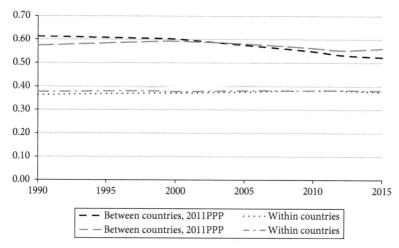

Figure 2.1 Global inequality (Gini), including China (black) and excluding China (grey), 1990–2015.

Source: Adapted from Edward and Sumner (2018), on the basis of household surveys.

As noted, the thesis that global inequality is falling is very much dependent on China's incredible development (a point made by others and systematically so by Niño-Zarazúa et al., 2014). It is evident from Figure 2.1 that the fall in between-country inequality is modest when China is excluded.

Figure 2.1 shows that if China is excluded from survey-based estimates of global inequality between countries, then global inequality in 2015 is only slightly lower than in 1990. One should not read this as implying that China's development is not important because clearly it is. However, due to the enormity of China's development, one may miss other important changes in the world outside China. Looking ahead, it is also worth noting that the contribution of China's development to falling global inequality may diminish over time.

The decline in global inequality is largely due to changes in inequality between countries. Figure 2.2 shows the extent to which the fall in global inequality has been driven by an important drop in the between-country component.

Anand and Segal, 2015). Anand and Segal (2017) assume that very rich households are simply excluded from surveys in order to incorporate top income data into their survey distributions (assuming the survey data represent the bottom 99 per cent of the population of each country). One question with this approach is how to extrapolate the data to the complete set of countries in the overall dataset. To do this, Anand and Segal estimate a relationship between the share of the top 10 per cent and the survey mean in the national survey distribution and other variables, and that of the top 1 per cent in the income tax data. They do not report estimates without China. Neither do Lakner and Milanović (2015) who have also attempted to adjust estimates of global inequality by a different method; namely, by assuming that discrepancies between survey data and national accounts data are entirely due to underreporting by the richest decile. Thus, they allocate the discrepancies to the top decile.

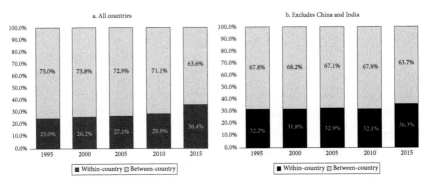

Figure 2.2 Trends in the components of global inequality, 1995–2015: Relative contribution of within- and between-country components to the mean log deviation. *Source*: Ortiz-Juarez and Sumner (2021).

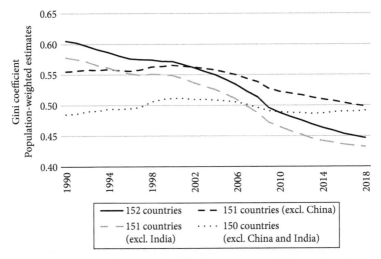

Figure 2.3 Global inequality (Gini), between-country component, national accounts data (2011PPP), population weighted, 1990–2018.
Source: Author's calculations based on per capita GDP from the IMF's World Economic Outlook Database (April 2019).

This finding is confirmed by an estimate of global inequality as inequality between countries' mean incomes using national accounts data, sometimes referred to as world or international inequality. Figure 2.3 shows that for a sample of 152 countries, global inequality between countries has markedly declined over time in population-weighted terms (and it has fallen in unweighted terms too). When taking the countries' population into account, it has declined from slightly above 0.60 to approximately 0.45 between 1990 and 2018. Figure 2.3 also shows that the trend of declining inequality apparent from the whole sample holds after removing China when using national accounts data. The trend of declining inequality also holds after removing India, though the fall is smaller over the period. However, the clear pattern of declining inequality apparent from the whole sample evaporates when excluding both China and India from the estimates based on national accounts data (see Figure 2.3). In fact, without China and India, global inequality between countries in 2018 is at similar levels as those observed in 1990 and actually rising again since the mid 2010s. This means the economic growth of all other developing countries even though positive for most developing countries had little impact on the between country aspect of global inequality.

In contrast, the second component of global inequality, within-country inequality, is surprisingly steady when aggregated. This is due to a 'scissor effect': national inequality rose in some countries while falling in others, at least as far as the survey-based estimates without top income adjustments tell us. Consequently, the two trends compensate one another when aggregated using survey-based estimates (see Edward and Sumner, 2018). Put simply, rising inequality in countries with relatively low initial inequality such as China and Indonesia, was counterbalanced at a global level by falling within-country inequality in countries with higher initial inequality in Latin American countries during the 2000s though it is not clear that this latter trend is likely to continue. Trends in national inequality are of course about political choices governments make.

The above does not mean that national inequality does not matter. Clearly it does matter, and intrinsic as well as instrumental reasons can be given as to why. Notably, at national level, there is typically a social contract or political settlement and governance structures of some kind (while none or poorly functioning ones exist at global level). It is though important to note that rising national inequality could yet become more widely evident as new top incomes data become available for a wide range of developing countries. Thus, this pattern of steady overall within-country inequality may not hold once further top-income data become available.

Moreover, looking ahead, as we discuss in Chapter 4, there are clear signs of rising pressure on within country *gross* income inequality, notably through the process of stalled industrialization and premature deindustrialization in a GVC world, via declining labour shares of income, and especially so for low-skilled workers.

One question is that of the convergence of incomes globally. For example, Patel et al. (2018) argue that since 1960, poorer countries have not grown faster than richer countries as the Solow growth model predicted. However, since about 1995, there was convergence for two decades. However, in absolute terms, Johnson and Papageorgiou (2020) revisit the last 50 years of data and find developing countries as a group have not been catching up with advanced nations in absolute terms. Further, actual convergence is such a long way in the future to beg the question of how to interpret trends. For illustration, if we consider the convergence of the GDP per capita of China with that of the US, we find that after 25 years of fast growth in per capita income, China's GDP per capita (2011 PPP) was just around a quarter of the GDP per capita of the US ($15,000 for China vs $55,000 for the US). If we ignore for a moment the COVID-19 pandemic then China could catch up by the late 2030s. However, the pandemic and its aftermath raise a big question mark over any such projections. Even prior to COVID-19 the most sophisticated long-run projections err on the side of caution (see e.g. Fouré et al., 2012). Moreover, if one ignores the COVID-19 pandemic and assumes that India grows exponentially and the US continues to grow linearly, then India could catch up with the GDP per capita (PPP) of the US around 2070. Even without the pandemic it would seem not plausible that a country would experience exponential growth rates for such a long period of time. These projections do, however, demonstrate that the assumptions that are needed to accept the eventual convergence—or the universality thesis to use Furtado's perspective—are implausibly optimistic.

In sum, since the 1960s and since the Cold War in particular, the developing world has shifted from a relatively homogenous group into a more heterogenous group of countries. At present, many developing countries are now in a situation where aid is not significant while a small set of developing countries are very poor and aid-dependent, perhaps so for many years to come. Furthermore, global inequality has fallen. However, this decline has been driven by the between-country component of inequality and China's as well as India's economic growth in particular.

2.3   The World's Two New Precarious 'Middles'

The bifurcation of the countries of the developing world has, as previously highlighted, also led to two burgeoning new 'middles': the first encompasses middle-income countries (MICs) which constitute the set of developing countries where aid is less significant. In these countries, some level of industrialization is generally evident. The second new 'middle' comprises people typically within those MICs who have moved out of poverty, at least when measured at very low consumption lines. However, those people are not sufficiently far from poverty lines as to have moved into security from future poverty. Hence, they are at risk of falling back into poverty. Indeed, it is these two new middles who now face, and are most at risk of, the consequences of stalled industrialization and premature deindustrialization which may slow growth.

In the late 1980s, the distribution of the world's countries and the world's people resembled what Quah (1996) called the 'twin peaks' of a polarized world. The distribution showed a hump at the poorer end (encompassing the countries and people living in the homogenous 'Third World'), a hump at the upper end (developed countries and their population), and weak prospects for convergence of the poorer group with the richer one. Since the 1990s, that twin-peaks world with a poorer and a richer hump has transitioned into one hump in the middle including the 'new middles' identified or 'twin middles' (to follow Quah's language) of countries and people of the contemporary world.

The first 'middle' of countries is the result of an expansion due to growth and evident in the number of countries officially classified by the World Bank as MICs (above about $1000 GNI per capita, Atlas method). The second middle comprises people who consume at levels above the global 'moderate' poverty line used by the World Bank (of $3.20 per day in 2011 PPP). A large proportion of these people still live well below the consumption lines associated with a permanent escape from poverty (estimated at approximately $13 per day in 2011 PPP by the World Bank, 2019a based on the method of López-Calva and Ortiz-Juarez, 2014; see also Sumner et al., 2014). The following paragraphs will initially discuss the first middle, referring to countries, and subsequently elaborate on the second middle, comprising people.

As noted, one quantification of the first middle—that of countries—is the official classification by the World Bank of MICs. Many countries are substantially above the World Bank's middle-income line, particularly the populous developing countries of China and India, whilst other developing countries are closer to the line. Figure 2.4 shows the number of low-, lower middle-, upper middle-, and high-income countries (respectively, LICs, lower MICs [LMICs], upper MICs [UMICs], and HICs) from 1987, when the World Bank classification began (and the classification is based on the GNI per capita, Atlas method not PPP conversion).

Each year's categorization is based on data collected two years before classification. Figure 2.4 illustrates the decline in the number of LICs since about 2000 to approximately 30 in 2018. Prior to that, the number of LICs had been rising (partly due to the economic collapse of the former Soviet Union and the transition post-Cold War in Eastern Europe). The number of HICs

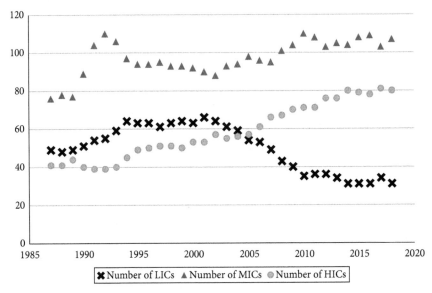

Figure 2.4   Number of countries by World Bank income group, 1987–2018.
Source: Author's estimates based on World Bank (2020).

(which currently are countries with approximately US$12,500 GNI per capita, Atlas method) has doubled from about 40 in 1990 to 80 in 2018.

At this point, one could simply dismiss all of this as a set of arbitrary lines, as indeed one could do with the declines in global poverty which we will come to shortly. However, as much in need of review the LIC/MIC/HIC lines are, they do record the substantial economic growth and also have symbolic meaning in terms of greater policy freedom in the form of greater access to substantial non-concessional finance, not only from the World Bank and IMF but also in the form of bond issues in private capital markets (which in contrast to donor conditionality are without policy conditions). Also, as crude as these lines are, they are, in the broadest sense, an aggregation of other development indicators, since cluster analysis (see Tezanos and Sumner, 2016) places all the remaining LICs in one homogeneous cluster. In fact, one justification for the continued use of these lines is that the remaining LICs are now relatively homogeneous in terms of their structural economic characteristics and a shared (weak) recent growth history. Moreover, almost all LICs are members of the United Nations (UN) grouping of least developed countries (LDCs). The new MICs, in contrast, are heterogeneous. They include many fast-growing 'emerging economies' where manufacturing-led growth is evident, such as China, though the 2000s commodity boom was important in some MICs. Many of these populous new MICs are home to a large proportion of the world's absolute poor at all poverty lines

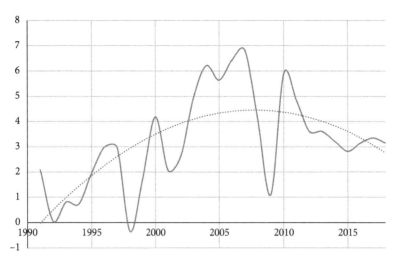

Figure 2.5 GDP per capita (constant prices) growth, annual average, all developing countries, 1990–2018.
Source: Author's estimates based on World Bank (2020).

(see discussion of poverty in MICs in Sumner, 2010, 2012, 2016). Some other countries, formerly planned economies, are 'bounce-back' new MICs that experienced economic collapse in the past but have grown back to MIC levels since (see the early 1990s MIC peak and fall in Figure 2.4). Although the economic growth in MICs is evident it is important to add such rapid economic growth rates in the developing world have waned since the mid-2000s (see Figure 2.5).

The other new 'middle' of people, we can define as comprising those people living on between $3.20 and $13 per day. We use $3.20 rather than the World Bank's $1.90 poverty line as the $1.90 is 'extreme' poverty and a very low line (see critical discussion of Fischer, 2018; Reddy and Lahoti, 2015). The data shows (Figure 2.6 and 2.7) that global poverty has fallen since the 1980s when measured at both the 'extreme' poverty line of $1.90 per day and poverty line of $3.20 per day.[5] However, outside of China, the fall in the number of people living in poverty is more modest. Moreover, many of these people living above $3.20 are still well below consumption lines associated with a permanent escape from poverty. Longitudinal studies estimate this line to be at $13 per day in 2011 PPP (World Bank, 2019a based on the method of López-Calva and Ortiz-Juarez, 2014; Sumner et al., 2014). This 'security from poverty' line can—very broadly—be seen as the line at which

---

[5] The former is the average poverty line in LICs. The latter is the average poverty line in LMICs. The average poverty line in UMICs is $5.50 per day.

people are very unlikely to fall back into absolute poverty. In other words, the risk of falling back below the $3.20 line diminishes to very low probability above $13 per day. This means that there is a substantial group of people living above the global absolute poverty lines but not sufficiently far to be certain of not falling back into poverty in the future. Figures 2.6 and 2.7 show daily consumption per capita of the global population and of the population of developing countries with and without China. When taking a poverty line of $13 per day, global poverty has not changed dramatically since the 1980s.[6] Global poverty measured at $13 per day has fallen from about 80 per cent of the world's population in the early 1980s to about 70 per cent in 2018. If we focus on the world excluding China less has changed since the early 1980s: In fact, in the world excluding China (see Figure 2.6, bottom) and in developing countries excluding China (see Figure 2.7, bottom) there is not that much change in terms of the level of poverty at $13 in almost 40 years.

What has happened? What has happened is that those moving out of poverty measured at $3.20 per day have not jumped in one leap to living above $13 per day even given this period accounts for four decades. Instead, they have moved into the precarious group with incomes between $3.20 and $13 per day (see Figure 2.6, top). This group between poverty and security has grown from just above 20 per cent of the world's population to about half of the world's population in 2018. In the developing countries excluding China the $3.20–$13 group (see Figure 2.7, bottom) has expanded to about half of the population of developing countries in 2018.

In short, we can sum up thus: In 2018, almost a quarter of the *entire* population of the developing world including China lived in absolute poverty (under $3.20 per day), about a fifth lived in security (over $13 per day), leaving the remainder—around a half of the developing world's entire population—in a precarious new middle (between $3.20 and $13 per day). This is the second new middle, the one of people who are neither day-to-day poor nor secure from the future risk of poverty.

How about at country level: Was Furtado right that on average just 5–10 per cent of the population each developing country would have incomes similar to citizens in the developed countries? Of course the answer will

---

[6] It is important to note that the data for 2015–2018 for India, which is home to most of the world's poor whatever the line taken, is contentious. The latest available extrapolated measure for poverty in India is for 2015. How exactly the poverty headcount in India changed between 2015 and 2018 is unclear. Felman et al. (2019) discuss the (leaked) report of India's National Sample Survey that had been withheld by the government (the long-standing survey has now been abandoned). The survey showed real consumption per capita had *fallen* by 3.7 per cent between 2011/12 and 2017/18. This figure sits uneasily with the official GDP growth data reported for the same period. In Figure 2.6 we use the 2015 data which means the figure overestimates poverty in India, 2015–2018 if India's GDP growth data is correct. On the other hand, if India's survey data is correct, Figure 2.6 under-estimates poverty 2015–2018.

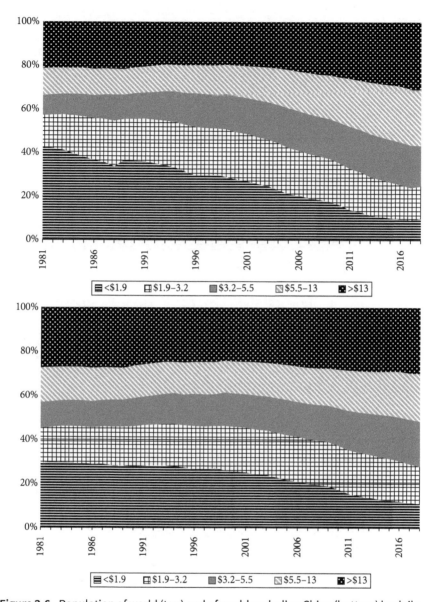

Figure 2.6 Population of world (top) and of world excluding China (bottom) by daily consumption per capita group, 1981–2018.
Source: Author's estimates based on World Bank (2020).

depend on what income line constitutes a non-poor life in advanced nations. One approach is to take the $13-per-day line though this would constitute a lifestyle whereby a person is living just above the income associated with a low risk of falling back into absolute poverty. More meaningful would be to take the average poverty line of richer countries—high income

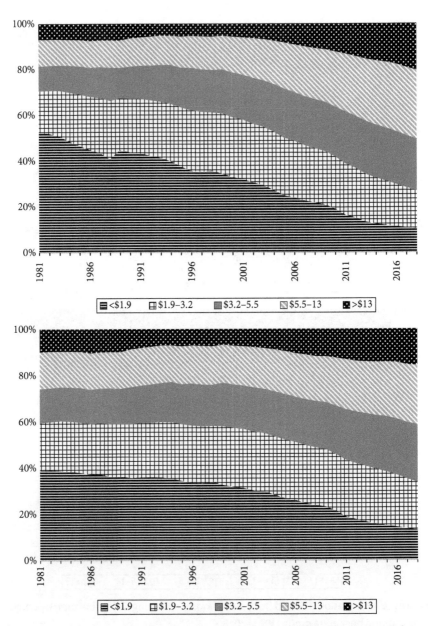

Figure 2.7 Population of all developing countries (top) and of developing countries excluding China (bottom) by daily consumption per capita group, 1981–2018.
Source: Author's estimates based on World Bank (2020).

countries—which is $21.70-per-day. Thus a non-poor person in an advanced country would have income above that level.

Table 2.2 shows the average poverty counts across developing countries when taking the average poverty lines of poorer countries, LICs, LMICs, and

Table 2.2 Mean (unweighted) poverty rates in developing countries (% of population under poverty line), 2018

Poverty line (per-day)	$1.90	$3.2	$5.5	$13	$21.70
LICs	0.45	0.70	0.88	0.98	1.00
MICs	0.08	0.19	0.39	0.75	0.89
All developing countries (LICs and MICs)	0.18	0.34	0.53	0.81	0.92

Note: Means are based on 103 developing countries with populations of over 1 million people in 2018 and available data.

Source: Author's estimates based on World Bank (2020); poverty lines are respectively, the average poverty lines of LICs, LMICs, UMICs, a security-from-future-poverty line, and HICs (see for details. López-Calva and Ortiz-Juarez, 2014; Ferreira and Sánchez-Páramo, 2017).

UMICs (respectively $1.90, $3.20, or $5.50 lines). Even at the $1.90 line, on average, one in five people in the countries of the developing world live in poverty. At the $3.20 line—on average—about one-third of people in the countries of the developing world live in poverty. The corresponding poverty counts at $5.50 and $13-per-day are higher, respectively half of the population and 80 per cent of the population. However, when one considers Furtado's prediction using the average poverty line of the advanced countries of $21.70 one finds that Furtado was startlingly close: even after 40 years of good economic growth in MICs, the population that would be non-poor in advanced nations is just 11 per cent; and for the entire developing world it is just 8 per cent of the population who would be non-poor in advanced countries.[7] In short, Furtado's prediction is surprisingly close even in MICs where there have been reasonable economic growth since the Cold War.

To be clear, in this section we are not making an argument that the income growth among the poorest people in the world has not been positive in general, rather that it has been slow and of a modest order and many people remain, in spite of four decades of good economic growth, below the income line associated with a permanent escape from absolute poverty. Further, the real issue is that setting and using very low poverty lines and communicating the trends based on these lines may lead to a narrative that absolute poverty is virtually eradicated or soon will be. What is presented in poverty measurement as a technical issue is actually highly political (see discussion in Edward and Sumner, 2019; Fischer, 2018). Global poverty reduction since the Cold War has been mostly about moving people from below to somewhat above a low poverty line. Highlighting this trend often ignites tempers and fierce

---

[7] Although on average across all MICs the poverty rates are in line with Furtado's forecast, there are some outliers, notably a handful of UMICs with poverty rates at $21.70 much lower than the average. There are six countries with $21.70 poverty rates below 70 per cent of population. These are Malaysia, Lebanon, Bosnia and Herzegovina, Costa Rica, Bulgaria, and Belarus.

debate but one cannot overlook the fact that absolute poverty has not fallen at more reasonable poverty lines, even with the impressive income growth in developing countries during the past two decades.[8]

In sum, since the end of the Cold War there has been a movement of people into what could be called a global precariat class. Absolute poverty has fallen when measured at the $3.20 line. Consequentially, a new middle has burgeoned of a population living between $3.20 and $13 which by 2018 accounted for about half of the developing world's population. One could liken this to a transition from global poverty towards global precarity.

Why does this all matter to stalling industrialization and the spectre of deindustrialization? First, it means that many of the countries which have achieved fast growth are likely to need new strategies in the face of stalling industrialization and deindustrialization to maintain economic growth and employment creation. Secondly, it means that many people are at risk of slipping back into poverty if growth were to weaken in middle-income developing countries, whether that is because of the economic shock of the COVID-19 pandemic and its aftermath or an economic slowdown due to stalled industrialization and premature deindustrialization.

2.4   The First Myth of Economic Development

The transformation due to substantial economic growth and the decline in importance of aid in much of the developing world is accompanied by a myth that economic development is ahistorical because developing countries have achieved so much progress. In this section it is argued that the prospects for national economic development are fundamentally framed by history and that late development is utterly different to earlier developers' experiences because global accumulation; the nature, extent, and reach of transnational corporations—or large companies to use Furtado's preferred term; and global finance are fundamentally different. This concept of late development, as noted, was clearly present—explicitly or implicitly—in the

---

[8] Whilst, on average, the poverty headcount falls and the incomes of the poorest rise in line with average income growth (see Dollar and Kraay, 2002; Dollar et al., 2013; Kraay, 2006), some recent contributions have reopened this debate with a focus on growth episodes with steady or rising poverty. Shaffer, Kanbur, and Sandbrook (2019, p. 40), for example, have noted that in up to a third of growth episodes poverty rates may not fall (based on the dataset used by Adams, 2004) and even in Dollar and Kraay's (2002) dataset, the incomes of the poorest quintile declined during positive mean survey income growth in 15 per cent of growth episodes (Donaldson, 2008). Furthermore, in Kraay's (2006) dataset the spells across 185 countries, many of which shorter than ten years, indicated the contribution of growth to poverty reduction to be between 43 per cent and 70 per cent, again suggesting changes in inequality should not be dismissed. We return to this discussion in Chapter 5.

contributions of early pioneers of post-WWII development economics, not only Celso Furtado but also others such as W. Arthur Lewis, Nicholas Kaldor, and Simon Kuznets, as well as other Structuralist and neo-Marxian scholars (see review in Sumner, 2018). However, important changes have become evident since the 1990s and are highly relevant to the forthcoming discussion of stalled industrialization and premature deindustrialization.

What does 'late development' mean precisely? To set a frame at the outset on what 'late development' means, we earlier referred to Gerschenkron (1962, p. 8) who argued that the pace and nature of economic development differs between 'pioneers' and 'latecomers' and that 'the opportunities inherent in industrialization…vary directly with the backwardness of the country'. In an essay and a later volume on relative backwardness, Gerschenkron (1962) argued that developing countries would have access to and develop with modern technology and thus develop at a faster speed than the early industrializers. Gerschenkron was optimistic that there were advantage[s] of backwardness in terms of adopting modern technology and thus speeding up economic development (see Selwyn, 2011 for a detailed discussion).

Furtado took the opposite view to that of Gerschenkron. Although Furtado agreed that 'industrialization in each era is shaped according to the degree of accumulation attained by the countries that lead the process, the relative effort required to take the first steps tend to increase over time' (2020 [1974], p. 11). Furtado argued that growth processes are different in developing (peripheral) countries and developed (centre) economies. Furtado (and many others) argued that developing countries are not just backward versions of developed economies but hybrid systems with two sectors, as briefly noted in the previous chapter: a 'nucleus' sector with modern technology and a 'backward' or pre-capitalist sector with little modern technology resonating, respectively, with the 'modern' and 'traditional' sectors of Lewis (1954).

The growth process, Furtado argued (like Lewis), is then driven by the movement of labour from the backward/traditional sector to the nucleus/modern sector because the movement of labour implies an increase in overall labour productivity of the economy. Furtado also argued that the level of underdevelopment is determined by the extent to which the backward sector dominates. As is very evident, Furtado's thinking on the dual economy follows that of Lewis (1954). There is also resonance with Myrdal's (1956, 1957a, 1957b) thinking on 'backwash and spread effects'.[9]

---

[9] Myrdal's major theoretical contribution was the interplay of 'backwash and spread effects' in global and regional economies, and in circular and cumulative processes, which exacerbated polarization. The backwash effect describes the phenomenon that as one area of a country develops, labour migrates to it,

Furtado (e.g. 1957, pp. 168–9) in fact cited the Lewis model and in personal correspondence that lamented that Furtado's group at CEPAL had not published a dual economy-type paper. That said he also critiqued the Lewis model as too optimistic.[10] Furtado (1958) used a two-sector model with a nucleus/modern and a backward/traditional sector to show the 'strangulation' of economic growth which he argued is due to the need to import investment goods in underdeveloped countries. Furtado argued that income concentration and external dependence would strangle both growth and the implied convergence that Gerschenkron foresaw unless there was an activist state. Gerschenkron did note (resonating with Furtado, Lewis, and others) that modernity and backwardness could live side-by-side. He argued as well that state planning was necessary to support infant industry. However, Gerschenkron made no reference to imperialism, neither in regard to how earlier developers' development was shaped by imperialism nor how imperialism added a layer of constraints to the process of late development for later developers (see Selwyn, 2011).

The existence of a backward/traditional/pre-capitalist sector was the distinctive feature of an underdeveloped country for Furtado (1964 [1961], 1983b [1978]), who defined the concept of dualism as the interdependence of the two modes of production, a capitalist and a non-capitalist mode. As per Lewis, the pre-capitalist sector acts as labour reserve and keeps wages low across the economy. For Furtado, the process of economic development employs imported technology from, and appropriate to, advanced countries. This leads to more capital-intensive production and increases in inequality given stable wages. For Lewis, the transfer of labour leads to capital accumulation, as profits are reinvested, and wages stay low. In contrast, for Furtado, the process reproduces the two sectors or 'structural duality' and leads to stagnation as the rate of profit falls because the internal markets size constrains economies of scale in the production of intermediate and capital goods. Industrialization thus stalls at the import-substitution phase. Furthermore, because the developed countries control advanced technology,

---

as does physical capital. That leaves a backward area that is worse off because of the movement than before the movement. Thus, growth in one area is to the detriment of another. In contrast, the spread effect describes the opposite trend when development in one area spreads to neighbouring areas.

[10]   Boianovsky (2007, p. 12) cites a letter from Furtado in 1955 as follows:

I call your attention to Lewis's work…I regard it as the best single piece ever written about the theory of development. He follows exactly the same approach adopted by us in our preliminary studies for planning techniques. I am convinced that if we had not been discouraged to 'theorize' at that stage, we would have been able to present two years ago the basic elements of a theory of development along the lines of this important contribution by Lewis. We are left with the fact that, having dedicated more time than any other person or group of people to think about and investigate in this field, we find ourselves today relatively behind and without anything of real significance to show.

developing countries are dependent. Specifically, there is a link between the internal process of exploitation and the 'external process of dependence'; if the latter increases, as it does during economic growth, the former will rise too (Furtado, 2020 [1974]).

Furtado was concerned with what produced underdevelopment and what perpetuated it. The nature of the type of technological change in developing countries was central:

> By orientating technological development towards labor-saving mechanisms which substitute labor for capital, the capitalist class could compensate for the tendency to relative labor scarcity and thereby preserve the social income-distribution scheme that existed when previous labor surpluses prevailed...Labor saving technology increases labor productivity in the sector that assimilates the technology at the same time that it expands the structural labor surplus...We must recognize...the great differences existing between the social transformations cause by the assimilation of technological progress in the underdeveloped countries and those that characterized the advance of capitalism in the countries that became industrialized since the last century...During the transformations of the present advanced capitalist economies, the problems resulting from group conflicts and class conflicts...have their solutions in the advance of technology itself...The current situation of the underdeveloped countries is, in a certain sense, the inverse: the ways in which technological innovation enters the economies generate problems with wide-ranging projections on the social level.
>
> (1970, pp. xx, xxii, xxiv–xxv)

Furtado (1954 [1952], 1957, 1963, 1965, 1970a, 1970b, 1973, 1983a, 2009 [1998]) viewed industrialization in Latin America—and developing countries more generally—as a process of stagnation and polarization. He specifically argued that industrialization polarizes, stratifies, and segments labour markets into one for formal employment of better paid, middle-class people and one for informal employment of less well paid, poorer people. This bifurcation means that Furtado questioned whether the Lewis turning point exists. He argued that in the Latin American case, modernization could start without economic development necessarily happening. Moreover, he posited that economic development *with* modernization was constrained because of the need to import capital goods and the constraint of market size (due to inequality). Similar to Lewis, Furtado argued that the traditional sector would act as a reserve of labour for the capitalist sector and given that the labour supply was nearly unlimited, real wages in the capitalist sector would remain just above whatever was possible to live on in the traditional sector.

Consumption was polarized between a small elite with rising incomes and the mass of population with low wages and stagnating standards of living. Furthermore, capital accumulation was accompanied by rising income inequality, increasing capital intensity, a shift towards capital-intensive sectors, and a shift towards luxury goods. This is how Furtado saw late development writing in the 1960s and 1970s. In short, the pool of surplus labour is reproduced and the Lewisian turning point delayed indefinitely.

How is late development to be understood in the contemporary global economy? How does the concept of late development provide a point of departure for theory that can explain global inequality and its persistence and reproduction? First, the technology of advanced nations continues to frame the development of late developers. For late developers, mature global industries with modern technology are not easy to access or can only be accessed on unfavourable terms of non-ownership or 'borrowing' that must be paid through patent and royalty fees due to intellectual property rights and typically via GVC participation. In fact, the *net* charges for use of intellectual property amounted to approximately $250bn per year by developing countries in 2018 (see Figure 2.8) and had grown rapidly since 1990 from a annual level of about $35bn per year (constant 2011 prices).

In short, late development implies structural disadvantage, not just temporal lateness. Moreover, late developers face competition with existing companies (and industries) that have well-established markets, networks, research and development centres, lower production costs per unit, and lower borrowing costs given established markets and rates of return.

Second, as Gerschenkron (1962) argued, each country case of industrialization is different because the global framework of industrialization has changed. In a similar vein, this book argues that China has industrialized under the novel conditions of a GVC world. In that process, the world has changed to such an extent that subsequent industrializers are unlikely to be able to follow that manufacturing pathway. This is because many industries that one would refer to as 'early industry' (in the sense that countries pursue those at an early stage of industrialization because they are labour-intensive, e.g. textiles and apparel) are now at much higher levels of productivity than they were pre-1990. This, coupled with future automation trends in manufacturing, means such early industries are likely to generate far fewer jobs than they did in the pre-1990 period. This points towards the end of late development as the pursuit of the industrial development model. In other words, pursuing industrialization gets harder and harder over time as more countries become industrialized. This is because new developers need to compete with the incumbents and because the global economy itself is different to earlier periods when other countries developed, leaving countries at

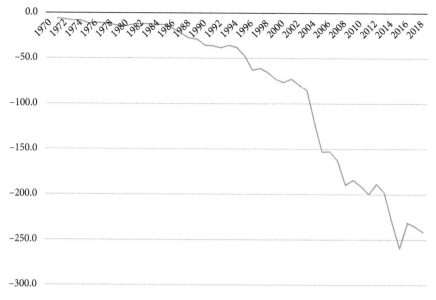

Figure 2.8   Net transfers (US$bn) for the use of intellectual property (developing countries minus high income countries), 1970–2018 (2011 constant US$).

Note: Net charges are LIC and MIC charges for use of intellectual property minus HIC charges for use of intellectual property.

Source: World Bank (2020) and adjusted to constant US$ (2011 prices).

a structural disadvantage. Each new late developer changes the playing field, leading Gerschenkron (1962, p. 44) to outline his 'general rule' of late industrialization as an 'orderly system of graduated deviations'.

Third, there have been very substantial changes in the nature of economic development. As noted in the introductory chapter and developed in the forthcoming chapters, the very meaning of industrialization has shifted from 'deep' to 'shallow' industrialization as a consequence of the emergence of a GVC world of fragmentated global production. 'Global value chains'—a term first coined in the mid-1990s by Gereffi (1994), who analysed the process of learning and upgrading for firms joining GVCs in the East Asian context— have become the basis of global production in which developing countries seek national economic development.[11]

Global trends in the expansion of GVCs overall show a steady rise from the mid-1990s to 2008, when the global financial crisis occurred. Then

---

[11]   Kaplinsky (2000, p. 8) provides a definition of GVCs as 'the full range of activities which are required to bring a product or service from conception, through the intermediary phases of production (involving a combination of physical transformation and the input of various producer services), delivery to final consumers, and final disposal after use'.

growth slowed and slightly declined from 2011 onwards (Timmer et al., 2014). It has been argued that the causes of this decline are a saturation of possibilities of production fragmentation, the reshoring of Chinese production as well as changes in demand and costs (Rodrik, 2018, p. 3). This saturation point is generating new economic and social consequences of GVC participation in middle-income developing countries as it sets limits on GVC-participation or the overall size of the pie that is to be competed over.

A 'shallow' form of industrialization—a diminished development—is based on GVC participation via domestic suppliers. As note developing countries are to specialize in particular stages of production and simply slot into GVCs where they have, or can develop, domestic suppliers. The higher-value activities—such as R&D, design, distribution, and advertising—tend to be at the beginning and end stages of production, and less likely to be situated in developing countries. In contrast, much developing country activity is—at best—likely to be in lower-value-adding assembly tasks—i.e. manufacturing, assembly, retail/sales—in the middle of GVCs. Consequently, GVC participation may help initially with shallow industrialization through some growth in both productivity and exports, but long-run or deep economic development may be curtailed (see Chapter 4). The benefits from GVC participation may be non-linear and initially accrue but then diminish or may even turn negative for employment or value-added in the longer-term.

Fourth, the historical pattern of structural transformation in earlier developers is now in question for late developers. In fact, it is likely to be harder than has been the case to achieve the well-known pathway of structural transformation (industrialization through manufacturing entire goods). Newer pathways (tertiarization) may occur at lower levels of per capita income than earlier developers experienced, with implications for employment growth, real-wage growth, and value-added.

The established pattern of structural transformation experienced by early developers was outlined in Clark, 1940; Chenery (1960), Chenery and Syrquin (1975), Kuznets (1965), and Syrquin (1988). That pattern is that (i) agriculture dominates employment and value-added at low levels of GDP per capita; (ii) shares of agriculture diminish as GDP per capita rises (to very low shares at high income); (iii) manufacturing has an inverted-U pattern in the sense that its shares are small at low GDP per capita levels and rise over time to a peak before falling again. One can add that at lower income levels, low-tech manufacturing such as food/beverages, textiles, and apparel develop, as these relate to basic human needs and are labour-intensive. As countries' income rise, the dominant subsectors evolve around resource-processing industry, such as basic and fabricated metals which are more capital-intensive. Subsequently, more technology-intensive manufactures, such as electrical machinery and apparatus, become dominant. Lastly, (iv) the service sector shares are low at low levels of GDP per capita and rise over time to very high levels at high GDP per capita. Duarte and Restuccia (2010, p. 135) empirically concur with the stylized history above and note that:

> All countries in the sample follow a common process of structural transformation. First, all countries exhibit declining shares of hours in agriculture, even the most advanced countries in this process, such as the United Kingdom and the United States. Second, countries at an early stage of the process of structural transformation exhibit a hump-shaped share of hours in industry, whereas this share is decreasing for countries at a more advanced stage. Finally, all countries exhibit an increasing share of hours in services.

However, this pattern—as we discuss in the next chapter—is under challenge, as many middle-income developing countries are experiencing the new pattern of economic development; namely, stalled industrialization, deindustrialization, and a tertiarization process.

In sum, the concept of late development remains useful to understand contemporary economic development as framed by the facts that some countries have achieved industrialization; that the modern technology of developed countries is imported by developing countries; that as every country industrializes it changes the global economy for the next country; that global production today is fragmented internationally, and that traditional structural transformation is becoming harder to sustain. The concept of late development is useful as it seeks to capture the historical context for developing countries pursuing economic development, and the bind that developing countries find themselves in because their development has been effectively stunted or diminished by historical events, not least colonization and late (re)industrialization itself.

In this book, 'late' is used to emphasize the historical context in which contemporary development takes place; specifically, that it occurs after some countries have already achieved industrialization and that late developers are competing in a radically different global economic context and against others who have had a huge head start. Thus, developing countries face a structural disadvantage. In short, the conceptual lens of late development as used in this book is intended to emphasize the difference between earlier and later development, and the different trajectories of countries depending on the timing of their economic development in global economic history.

2.5   Conclusion

This chapter has discussed the first 'great transformation' since the Cold War—of substantial economic growth and the falling significance of aid—and the consequential emergence of two new middles in the developing world. The chapter has thus situated the forthcoming discussion of stalled industrialization and premature deindustrialization within the broader landscape of economic development and the bifurcation of the developing world especially since the Cold War.

We can establish a set of observations or stylized facts as Kaldor would have. First, two precarious new middles have emerged, one of countries and one of people in the developing world. If stalled industrialization and premature deindustrialization imply weaker and unequalizing economic growth and/or weaker employment growth, then the new middle-income countries will face stagnation in terms of growth and the new middle precariat class may fall back into poverty if employment opportunities in manufacturing evaporate due to the longer-term process of stalled industrialization.

A second Kaldorian stylized fact is that of the underlying dynamic of the tectonic movements as discussed in this chapter. That is, new modes of structural transformation—stalled industrialization, deindustrialization, and tertiarization—have become prevalent in much of the developing world. The COVID-19 pandemic will likely act as accelerator in terms of tertiarization and the stalling of industrialization, as manufacturing GVCs in middle-income countries are disrupted by lockdowns, inputs will become costlier to source, and recessions will lead to layoffs.

In sum, this chapter has outlined the bifurcation of the developing world and the emergent two new middles. The chapter has argued that the myth of economic development as ahistorical is untenable. The lens of late development provides a conceptual basis with which one can build a theory of the persistence of global inequality. In the next chapter we turn to discuss 'new' patterns of economic development emerging.

3
Contemporary Structural Change

Stalled Industrialization and the Spectre of Premature
Deindustrialization

3.1 Introduction

This chapter discusses contemporary patterns of economic development.
The chapter focuses on the second great transformation since the Cold War.
Specifically, the emerging phenomena of stalled industrialization and premature deindustrialization in the developing world. The chapter also discusses the myth accompanying this second transformation: that economic
development is sector-neutral. The chapter argues that manufacturing
remains superior as the lead sector for economic development due to manufacturing's ability to generate substantial value-added *and* formal employment growth.

In the previous chapter, we discussed the outcome of the bifurcation of the
developing world into two new precarious middles. The first one refers to the
set of fast-growing middle-income developing countries where aid is less
relevant and where some degree of industrialization is evident. The second
new middle consists of people within those MICs who have moved out of
poverty, at least when measured at low poverty lines, but who have not
moved sufficiently far to be secure from risk of future poverty. It is thus the
two new middles who now face, and are most at risk of, the consequences of
stalled industrialization and the threat of premature deindustrialization.

In Chapter 2, we argued that the concept of late development provides a
point of departure for a theory of the persistence and reproduction of global
inequality. In this chapter, we discuss the processes of stalled industrialization and the spectre of premature deindustrialization. We identify an evolution from an 'old' to a 'new' form of economic development. Specifically, the
shift from industrialization to stalled industrialization or deindustrialization
and tertiarization. We argue that stalled industrialization and premature
deindustrialization will have major consequences for the two middles, as
these processes exacerbate global income inequality, between and within

Deindustrialization, Distribution, and Development: Structural Change in the Global South. Andy Sumner, Oxford University Press.
© Andrew Sumner 2021. DOI: 10.1093/oso/9780198853008.003.0003

countries. This is because the economic development in developing countries that will be engendered by stalled industrialization and premature deindustrialization will mean a slower narrowing of the gap between developing and advanced countries, as economic growth is likely to be slower. This new mode of economic development is also likely to be associated with immiserizing growth. This means growth with falling labour shares and thus upwards pressure on national income inequality; growth with weak employment growth in the modern or nucleus sector; and growth accompanied by labour transition from the more equal, formalized sector (where relative pay and conditions are better) to the less equal, informalized sector.

In this chapter, the theses are as follows: first, that a new pathway of structural transformation and economic development is emerging. The data show that the premature deindustrialization thesis *is* confirmed in the shares of employment for all and for formal manufacturing; and value-added shares accounted for formal manufacturing (i.e. the Lewisian modern or GVC-world integrated manufacturing sector). In terms of the experience of current developing country we find that the contemporary period is—on average—one of stalled industrialization but not (yet) deindustrialization of employment; and stalled industrialization and signs of deindustrialization of value-added in the formal sector; though amid growing shares in all manufacturing. It is important to note that these are average trajectories, and a small number of developing countries could buck the average trend.

The trends are consistent with the thesis that stalled industrialization and deindustrialization will exacerbate the between-country component of global inequality. Furthermore, the myth accompanying this second transformation—that economic development is sector-neutral—is flawed. This chapter argues that stalled industrialization and deindustrialization in developing countries matter. We build on the previous discussion on the late development concept to discuss the 'special' aspects of manufacturing in terms of value-added and employment growth.

The chapter is structured as follows: Section 3.2 discusses the varieties of economic development in terms of structural transformation with a focus on manufacturing. Section 3.3 then assesses the empirics across developing countries. Section 3.4 is concerned with the myth accompanying stalled industrialization and deindustrialization—that economic development is sector-neutral—and underlines why stalled industrialization and the spectre of premature deindustrialization matter for developing countries. Section 3.5 concludes.

3.2 Varieties of Economic Development and the 'New' Normal

In Chapter 2, we referred to the well-trodden pattern of structural transformation. Specifically, the one outlined historically (see Clark, 1940; Chenery, 1960; Chenery and Syrquin, 1975; Kuznets, 1965; Syrquin, 1988) and empirically confirmed by Duarte and Restuccia (2010). The traditional pattern is based on the stylized picture that agriculture shares of value-added and employment fall as GDP per capita rises, that manufacturing follows an inverted-U pattern as GDP per capita rises, and that services rise over time to high levels at higher GDP per capita. That said, stalled industrialization and the spectre of premature deindustrialization raise questions over this pattern of structural transformation. In this section, we argue that 'old' structural transformation that shaped the pre-1990 period has been replaced with a 'new' mode of structural transformation in the form of stalled industrialization or deindustrialization and tertiarization.

How are developing countries supposed to achieve economic development? This has been a core question of development economics since the emergence of the field as a distinct area of enquiry and is evident in the work of early pioneers of development economics such as Furtado, Lewis, Kaldor, Kuznets, and many others including the likes of Rosenstein-Rodan (1943) and Nurkse (1953), Myrdal (1956, 1957a, 1957b), and Schumpeter (1942) too. The question of economic development has typically been defined as how to induce a shift from a low-productivity, agrarian society to a higher productivity, manufacturing economy. In Furtado's or Lewisian terms, the question is how to start and maintain an on-going shift of labour from the traditional/backward sector to the modern/nucleus sector.

Sectors and their inherent differences were an absolutely core aspect of theorizing in early development economics and remain so in some but not all contemporary economic development theory. In the classical school approach—represented by Furtado, Lewis, Kaldor, and Kuznets, among others—economic development is driven by changing structures of GDP and employment that lead to productivity growth. The inter-sectoral view of economic development dates back to classical political economy (see Heintz, 2010 for discussion). Since the productivity rates between sectors differ so substantially, the transfer of labour is a major source of productivity gains and thus economic growth.

The Lewis dual economy model (see notably, 1954, 1955, 1958, 1969, 1972, 1976, 1979) that, as noted in the previous chapter, has much in common with Furtado's thinking though with some differences, is one of the best-known models of economic development in developing countries. Although over sixty years old in its earliest iteration, the model remains relevant today to developing countries (see Gollin, 2014 for contemporary discussion). The dual model provides a heuristic device or an ideal type, in the Weberian sense, for thinking about structural transformation and economic development with an emphasis on labour, which is the factor of production that dominates developing countries.

To recap and expand, Lewis argued that the driver of capital accumulation was a sectoral movement of labour from the 'traditional', 'non-capitalist', or 'informal' sector (Furtado's backward sector) to the 'modern', 'capitalist', or 'formal' sector (Furtado's nucleus sector). The 'traditional' sector is characterized by low productivity, low wages, and, as prices are determined by the average product instead of the marginal product, by widespread disguised unemployment. The 'modern' sector is distinguished by higher productivity while its wages are set by productivity and the wages in the traditional sector. Crucial is the existence of surplus labour in the traditional sector. Because of surplus labour, wages are set just above subsistence across the whole economy. This leads to the transfer of labour over time from the traditional to the modern sector and to capitalists capturing profits (in the form of labour productivity gains above wages and other costs). These are the source of growth via reinvestment. The floor for wages is set at subsistence. When the surplus labour disappears, an integrated labour market and economy emerge and consequently, real wages start to rise. Lewis was more optimistic than Furtado, as he argued that economic development would be propelled by the labour transition. In contrast, Furtado saw stagnation and no Lewisian turning point.

The Lewis model, like Furtado's dualism, was intended as a critique of the neoclassical approach in two aspects. First, Lewis argued that labour was available to the modern sector of an economy not in a perfectly elastic supply but upward sloping (rather than flat). Relatedly, Lewis (see 1958, pp. 8, 18) also made a distinction between productive labour, which produced a surplus, and unproductive labour, which did not. Second, Lewis also rejected the neoclassical assumptions of perfect competition, market clearing, and full employment.

There have been various critiques of the Lewis model, many of which are of a 'red herring' variety as Ranis (2004, p. 716) puts it, meaning they are easily responded to or actually critiques of Lewisians rather than the writings of Lewis himself. Many relate to the assumption of labour abundance in the subsistence sector (and thus the dominance of that sector's wage rate across the entire economy) and the emergence of the urban informal sector, although Lewis' conception of surplus labour explicitly included the urban informal sector (see discussion in Fei and Ranis, 1964; Harris and Todaro, 1970; Minami, 1973; Schultz, 1964; Rosenzweig, 1988; Todaro, 1969).

A set of contemporary challenges throws up greater levels of complexity. First, domestic labour migration may not be permanent but circular (back-and-forth) or 'commuting'. Second, the contemporary scale of inter-sectoral resource flows via the growth of remittances further blurs the line between sectors. Finally, the Lewis transition can take a variety of forms beyond the one anticipated by Lewis and it is by no means guaranteed that the transfer will be from low- to high-productivity activities as flagged by McMillan and Rodrik (2011). Indeed, the opposite can be the case if there is a labour transfer from high productivity manufacturing to low productivity tertiary sectors.

Kim and Sumner (2019) present a typology of varieties of structural transformation with a focus on what is happening in the modern manufacturing sector. They identify patterns of traditional industrialization—'primary' and 'upgrading' industrialization—which entails the movement of labour from the traditional sector to the modern—manufacturing—sector and patterns of 'new' economic development, which may entail the shift of labour from the modern—formal manufacturing—sector to the traditional—e.g. informal services—sector, namely, stalled industrialization and deindustrialization. The typology is based on empirical trends in manufacturing value-added and employment shares. The categorization has been constructed based on the recent *direction of changes* in the manufacturing shares and not on the absolute *levels* of those shares. A country with a lower manufacturing share may be categorized as going through industrialization whereas a country with a higher manufacturing share may be categorized as experiencing deindustrialization. In each case, five-year moving averages of manufacturing value-added and employment shares are used in order to smooth out annual fluctuations and find meaningful trends. Figure 3.1 shows a stylized depiction of each of the varieties of structural transformation by plotting manufacturing shares of employment against manufacturing value-added shares.

It is important to note that not all developing countries fit neatly into this typology. More precisely, these varieties are not suited for the poorest, aid-dependent developing countries that remain largely agrarian or those heavily dependent on the mining sector. A separate analysis is needed for these countries. It is also important to note that countries are *not* fixed within the variety of structural transformation to which this analysis has assigned them. Shifting between different varieties is possible and, in some cases, desirable. Table 3.1 compares each variety with an exemplar; specifically, India, China, Indonesia, and Brazil. Figures 3.2 to 3.5 then show manufacturing shares

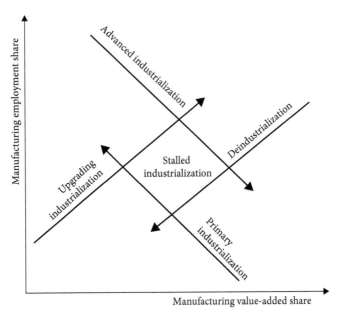

Figure 3.1 Varieties of industrialization and deindustrialization.
Source: Figure developed from Kim and Sumner (2019).

(left) and manufacturing labour productivity (right) for each exemplar of structural transformation.

In terms of Lewisian movements, India is the exemplar of *primary industrialization*. In India, we can see three distinct periods of manufacturing trends. The first period from 1980 to the late 1990s was characterized by rising shares of both value-added and employment shares, yet this increase was not dramatic. This was followed by a second period of rising employment shares accompanied by falling value-added shares. More specifically, from the late 1990s, the value-added shares reversed their course and declined, followed by a stagnation at around 17 per cent in the second half of the 2000s. In contrast, the manufacturing employment shares continued to rise gradually until the mid-2000s and then stayed at around 12 per cent in the second half of the 2000s. The third period starting in the late 2000s portrayed an opposite trend of rising value-added shares but declining employment shares. Consequently, India's industrialization between 1990 and 2010 was more evident in employment shares than in value-added shares, thus it is defined as primary—meaning labour-intensive—industrialization. Consistent with this pattern, we can see a stagnating international competitiveness in labour manufacturing productivity in India vis-à-vis the US during the first period. Labour manufacturing productivity vis-à-vis the US then fell dramatically in the second period before recovering sharply during the third.

Table 3.1 Varieties of industrialization and deindustrialization in developing countries

Variety	Primary industrialization	Upgrading industrialization	Stalled industrialization	Premature deindustrialization
Manufacturing value-added share	Peaked	Not peaked	Plateauing	Peaked
Manufacturing employment share	Not peaked	Not peaked	Plateauing	Peaked
Recent trend in relative to the US manufacturing productivity	Stagnating	Increasing	Declining	Declining
Exemplar in current period	India	China	Indonesia	Brazil

Note: If the highest level of value-added or employment shares since 1980 was recorded during 2005–2010, then the shares are regarded as 'not peaked'. If the highest shares were recorded during 1980–2004, then the shares are regarded as 'peaked'. 'Advanced industrialisation' not included in table as refers to developed countries.

Source: Kim and Sumner (2019) based on data from the GGDC 10-Sector Database (Version 2015).

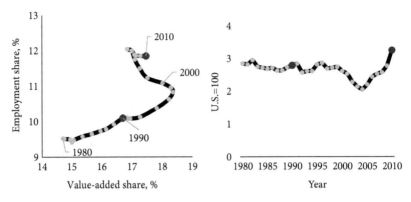

Figure 3.2 India's manufacturing shares (left) and manufacturing labour productivity (right), 1980–2012.

Source: Kim and Sumner (2019) based on the GGDC 10-Sector Database (Version 2015) and IMF World Economic Outlook Database (2019).

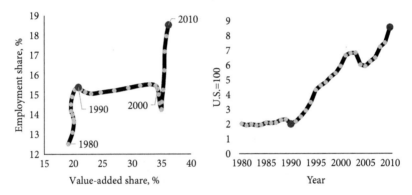

Figure 3.3 China's manufacturing shares (left) and manufacturing labour productivity (right), 1980–2012.

Source: Kim and Sumner (2019) based on the GGDC 10-Sector Database (Version 2015) and IMF World Economic Outlook Database (2019).

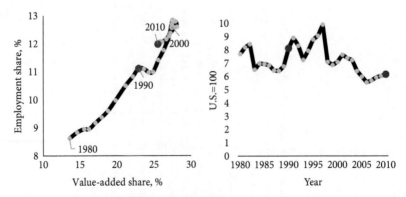

Figure 3.4 Indonesia's manufacturing shares (left) and manufacturing labour productivity (right), 1980–2012.

Source: GGDC 10-Sector Database (Version 2015) and IMF World Economic Outlook Database (2019).

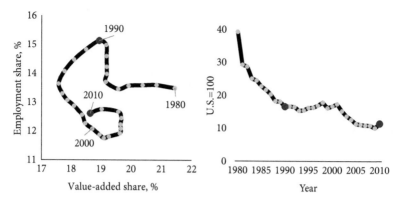

Figure 3.5 Brazil's manufacturing shares (left) and manufacturing labour productivity (right), 1980–2012.
Source: GGDC 10-Sector Database (Version 2015) and IMF World Economic Outlook Database (2019).

Next, in terms of a Lewisian movement, China exemplifies—par excellence—*upgrading industrialization*. We can observe three distinct periods of manufacturing trends. During the first period from 1980 to 1990, employment shares rose steeply while value-added shares barely changed and remained at around 20 per cent. The second period from 1990 to 2000 demonstrated an opposite trend with employment shares barely growing and value-added shares increasing dramatically from 21 per cent in 1990 to 34 per cent in 2000. The third period from 2000 to 2010 showed another sudden spurt in employment shares, accompanied by steady value-added shares. As a result of these trends, both value-added and employment shares were substantially higher in 2010 compared to 1990. During the first period, the data indicates flat international competitiveness in terms of labour productivity in manufacturing in China vis-à-vis productivity in the US. The second period showed an impressive jump, followed by a lull and another notable rise in the third period.

Indonesia is the exemplar of *stalled industrialization*. The data shows two periods. During one long period from 1980 to the late 1990s (up to the Asian financial crisis), both employment and value-added shares increased rapidly. However, the increasing trend suddenly stopped in the late 1990s. The shares stagnated during the first half of the 2000s before starting to decline in the mid-2000s. Hence, in 2000, a second period of falling employment and value-added shares started. It is this period where stalled industrialization is evident. As a result, the shares in 2010 were similar to those in the mid-1990s. International competitiveness in labour productivity in manufacturing vis-à-vis the US proved rather volatile and stagnated over the years with a particularly notable fall around 2000.

Finally, in terms of Lewisian movements, Brazil serves as an exemplar of *premature deindustrialization*. Brazil experienced a visible decline in the value-added shares in the first half of the 1980s, accompanied by steady employment shares. This was followed by an increase in the employment shares in the second half of the 1980s, combined with stagnant value-added shares. Between 1990 and 2010, the changes in value-added and employment shares showed varied patterns over time, but the shares generally declined, resulting in both shares being lower in 2010 than in 1990. A large decline in the value-added shares during the early 1990s was recovered in the following decade, but the shares declined again during the second half of the 2000s. Employment shares consistently decreased during the 1990s before plateauing at around 12 per cent during the 2000s. Consequently, from 1990 onwards, premature deindustrialization becomes clear. Brazil's labour productivity in manufacturing versus the US is striking since it declines dramatically from 40 per cent of the productivity of the US in 1980 to just 10 per cent of that of the US in 2010.

The distinct trends across these four exemplars illustrate how much the question of economic development can differ. For India, the major challenge is to sustain labour-intensive primary industrialization for some time to absorb the expanding labour force and devise a strategy to bring forward the transition to upgrading industrialization. For China, the major goal is to accelerate the process of upgrading industrialization and prepare for the economic and social consequences of phasing out labour-intensive manufacturing as the country seeks to enter the phase of advanced industrialization. For Indonesia, the challenge is to return to the upgrading industrialization it experienced before the late 1990s. A failure to do so would mean the beginning of premature deindustrialization. For Brazil, policies are needed to shift the country towards advanced industrialization. In short, these four exemplar countries illustrate the different varieties of structural transformation outlined. Next, we broaden the empirical focus to consider industrialization and deindustrialization across developing countries and the extent to which the new varieties of structural transformation identified above are evident in the 'average' developing country.

3.3 The Cross-Country Empirics of Industrialization and Deindustrialization

Existing studies of industrialization and deindustrialization point towards an empirically observed rupture in the relationship between manufacturing and economic development around 1990. New varieties of structural transformation—stalled industrialization and deindustrialization—have occurred in many middle-income developing countries in the post-1990 period. Rodrik (2016) demonstrates that trends in manufacturing employment are statistically different in the two periods. Furthermore, Haraguchi et al. (2019) illustrate that the two periods also vary statistically in terms of the drivers of successful industrialization. In short, something has happened that has changed the nature of global manufacturing and that is the emergence of a GVC-world.[1]

A set of cross-country papers has explored industrialization and deindustrialization in the developing world. These studies generally use a similar methodological approach to each other, namely regression analysis to outline the pattern of structural transformation (e.g. Amirapu and Subramanian, 2015; Atolia et al., 2020; Dasgupta and Singh, 2006; Felipe et al., 2018; Felipe and Mehta, 2016; Frenkel and Rapetti, 2012; Herrendorf et al., 2013; Palma, 2005, 2008; Pieper, 2000; Rodrik, 2016; Szirmai and Verspagen, 2011; Tregenna, 2009, 2014). There is also a set of single-country case studies though these are difficult to compare insofar as they deploy different definitions, methodology, and methods (e.g. for Malaysia, see Henderson and Phillips, 2007; Rasiah, 2011; Tan, 2014; for Indonesia, see Manning and Purnagunawan, 2017; for Mexico, see Cruz, 2014; for Chile, see Gwynne, 1986; for Pakistan, see Hamid and Khan, 2015; and for Brazil, see Cypher, 2015 and Jenkins, 2015b).

The cross-country and single country papers have focused on the pattern of structural transformation and the question of premature deindustrialization in developing countries. Put simply, premature deindustrialization occurs when: (i) the manufacturing sector peaks at *lower shares* of employment and/or value-added than was historically the case for earlier industrializers; and/or (ii) the manufacturing sector peaks *at lower levels of income per capita* than was historically the case for earlier industrializers. In other words, the developmental opportunities that manufacturing presents are being exhausted earlier, and with fewer of the social and economic benefits that have typically accrued to countries through manufacturing development.

In order to assess in-depth we consider the empirics. We take the manufacturing employment share (as a share of the total employment) and manufacturing output which is measured as the value-added (as a share of GDP)

---

[1] We continue using the 1990 cut-off in the analysis throughout this book for conceptual and empirical reasons. Conceptually, the 1990 line marks the political changes of the end of the Cold War, technological changes induced by the information and communications technology (ICT) revolution that took off in the 1990s, and most importantly the economic changes of trade and investment liberalization which created a GVC-world in the post-1990s era (that were nascent prior to 1990).

in constant prices. We estimate measures with three databases for the following sub-samples: the full sample (all countries); developed countries (countries which are high-income countries (HICs)); developing countries (current low-income countries (LICs) and MICs)); as well as developing and former developing countries combined, henceforth labelled 'developing and former' (LICs, MICs, and countries which have become HICs post-1990 but would not have been classified as 'developed countries' prior to 1990 based on a range of indicators).

We follow the approach of Rodrik (2016). See Sumner (2021). for full details. The analysis presented in this book is, as discussed in Chapter 1, is an approach based on Kaldorian methodology. To recap from Chapter 1, statistics are 'always subject to numerous snags and qualifications' as Kaldor (1961, pp. 177–8) put it. Thus, the discussion is one of longer-term trends, patterns, and regularities, or a quantitative economic history in the Kuznetsian sense in order to make observations, develop stylized facts, and use these to build theory.

In considering the data, we find nuances in revisiting the individual datasets in contrast to the merged datasets used in many of the other studies in this area. First, we find that the premature deindustrialization thesis *is* confirmed for employment shares and value-added shares though the latter, value-added is only for formal manufacturing. Secondly, however, we find that on average, the trend in developing countries is one of stalled industrialization—not—as far as time the data covers—deindustrialization of employment; and stalled industrialization and indications of deindustrialization of value-added in the formal sector; though amid growing shares in all manufacturing. These findings imply that deindustrialization is happening in the formal, i.e. GVC-integrated, modern/nucleus sector. The findings also imply that the informal manufacturing sector—itself a traditional sector in Lewis/Furtado terms—may to some extent be acting as an employment 'sponge', as labour shifts from formal to informal manufacturing when there is less activity in the formal manufacturing sector. Whatever the precise pattern, these effects are clearly linked to a GVC-world since it is on average formal manufacturing that is deindustrializing in developing countries. Furthermore, stalling industrialization and deindustrialization are tied to the emergence of a GVC-world post-1990 because it is the post-1990 period that exhibits the pattern.

We use three datasets: to recap, the Groningen Growth and Development Centre (GGDC) 10-Sector Database, Version 2015; the UNIDO INDSTAT-2 dataset, Version 2019; and the UNSD National Accounts Main Aggregates Database, December 2018 Version. Table 3.2 outlines details on the datasets

Table 3.2 Datasets used

Dataset, years coverage, and reference	Variable	Number of countries (and observations)			
		Full sample	Developed countries	Developing and former developing countries	Developing countries
The Groningen Growth and Development Centre (GGDC) 10-Sector Database, 2015 Version 1950–2012 See Timmer, de Vries, and de Vries (2015)	Employment shares	42 (2210)	15 (810)	31 (1590)	27 (1400)
	Value-added shares	41 (2255)	14 (802)	31 (1664)	27 (1453)
UNIDO INDSTAT-2, 2019 version 1963–2017 See UNIDO (2019)	Employment shares	140 (3933)	51 (1808)	93 (2252)	89 (2125)
UNSD National Accounts Main Aggregates Database, 2018 version 1970–2017 See UNSD (2018)	Value-added shares	220 (9615)	70 (3150)	154 (6657)	150 (6465)

Note: Population and GDP per capita are taken from the Penn World Table Version 9.1 (see Feenstra, Inklaar, and Timmer, 2015).
Source: Author's elaboration.

and samples. It is worth noting some further important differences between the datasets in addition to earlier observations. The GGDC 10-Sector dataset defines employment as the total persons engaged ('all persons employed' including all paid employees but also self-employed and family workers) and it is constructed with population censuses combined with labour force and business surveys which allows the construction of inter-census trends. The sector categories are comparable. It also includes informal employment in principle.[2]

In contrast, the UNIDO INDSTAT-2 defines employment as all persons engaged except working proprietors, active business partners, and unpaid family workers. It is constructed by UNIDO from national sources as well as from national governmental sources provided by the Organisation for Economic Co-operation and Development (OECD) and the UNSD. It is based on the *formal* manufacturing sector. UNIDO's data come from national industrial surveys and censuses as well as from samples of formal sector manufacturing establishments. These surveys typically exclude small-scale and informal establishments. Depending on the survey, it might cover firms with at least five, or ten, formally employed workers.[3] The UNSD National Accounts Main Aggregates Database is also constructed from national sources and based on the formal manufacturing sector.

In this book, we make an assumption that the GGDC employment data cover *all* manufacturing (formal and informal sectors) and the GGDC value-added do so too to some reasonable extent. As Daio et al. (2017) note, the extent to which the value-added data cover all manufacturing depends on national sources. In contrast, both UN datasets, UNIDO (employment data) and UNSD (value-added data) cover the *formal* manufacturing sector only. An important qualification is that informality/formality differ slightly between employment and value-added as the latter is based on the scale of enterprise.

If we analyse the data, what do we find? In Figures 3.6 to 3.9 the vertical axis indicates manufacturing shares (of employment or value-added) and

---

[2] Diao et al. (2017, pp. 4–6) note that: (i) the data broadly include all employment regardless of formality or informality, but the extent to which the value-added data do so depends on the quality of national sources (see Timmer et al., 2015); (ii) the quality of data from poor countries and Africa in particular is questioned, though it is noted that Gollin et al. (2014) have shown high correlations between national accounts data and sectoral measures of consumption, which is reassuring; moreover, the African countries in the GGDC dataset are those with the strongest national statistical offices; (iii) the measurement of labour inputs is not by hours but by the number of employees in a sector. Thus seasonality might lead to an underestimation of labour productivity in agriculture, for example, though Duarte and Restuccia (2010) find a correlation between hours worked and employment shares in a set of 29 developed and developing countries.

[3] Additionally, the measurement of labour inputs is not by hours but by the number of employees in a sector.

the horizontal axis shows GDP per capita in log scale. The figures show employment and value-added shares of manufacturing using GGDC, UNIDO, and UNSD datasets for the four sub-samples—the country groupings— previously outlined. We plot the 'average' country in the sub-sample.[4]

We can make a set of empirical observations or stylized facts.[5] First, on premature deindustrialization, what can we say on the thesis of premature deindustrialization in terms of the peak of manufacturing shares and the turning point of the inverted-U in income per capita vis-à-vis earlier industrializers? First, employment shares: Figures 3.6 and 3.7 illustrate the premature deindustrialization thesis in that they show a lower peak of employment shares for developing/former countries (post-1990) and at a lower GDP per capita than developed countries' peak (pre-1990) in both *all* and *formal* manufacturing. The turning point is premature in terms of employment shares and per capita income. Second, value-added shares: Figures 3.8 and 3.9 shows that the premature deindustrialization thesis is however not confirmed

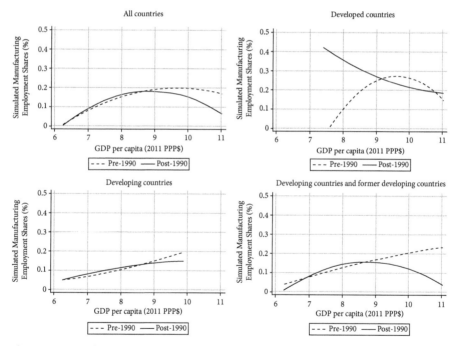

Figure 3.6 Simulated manufacturing employment shares, pre-/post-1990, GGDC dataset.

Source: Author based on GGDC 10-Sector database.

---

[4] These figures directly follow the approach of Rodrik (2016, p. 6) and plot a simulated curve which represents the median country in the sample.

[5] For further discussion on data, estimates underlying figures and findings see Sumner et al. (2021).

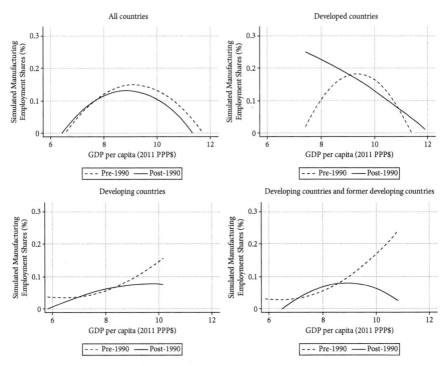

Figure 3.7 Simulated manufacturing employment shares, pre-/post-1990, UNIDO dataset.
Source: Author based on UNIDO INDSTAT2 database.

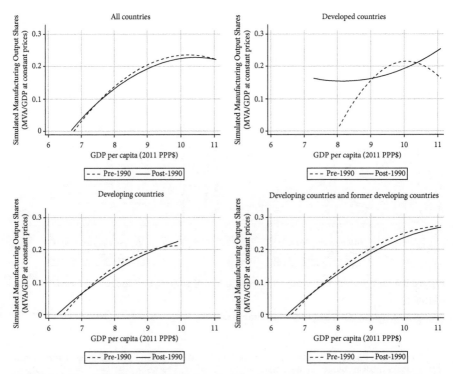

Figure 3.8 Simulated manufacturing output shares, pre-/post-1990, GGDC dataset.
Source: Author based on GGDC 10-Sector database.

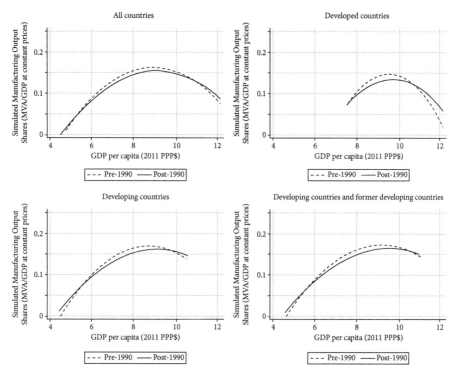

Figure 3.9 Simulated manufacturing output shares, pre-/post-1990, UNSD dataset.
Source: Author based on UNSD national accounts database.

for value-added shares in *all* manufacturing. The picture regarding *formal* manufacturing shares for the developing/former sub-sample versus the developed countries is as follows: the peak of value-added shares occurs at a similar turning point for developing/former countries as that for developed countries (pre- or post-1990). The turning point is though earlier, though not by a large amount, in terms of per capita income for developed/former (vis-à-vis developed countries). In sum, premature deindustrialization *is* (i) evident in all and formal sector employment; (ii) not evident in all manufacturing value-added shares though there are indications in formal value-added of the earlier turning point.

Second, on contemporary trends we can note a further set of stylized facts regarding the emergence of a GVC-world, post-1990. First, employment shares: Figure 3.6 depicts simulated manufacturing shares of employment and compares the pre-1990 and the post-1990 period using the Groningen Growth and Development Centre (GGDC) dataset (i.e. all manufacturing, formal and informal). The data show how the post-1990 period differs to the pre-1990 period. For illustration, in the developing countries group, an upward curve pre-1990 has become a plateauing curve post-1990. In the developing and former grouping, the curves show that an initial process of industrialization pre-1990 has become an inverted-U shape and premature deindustrialization has set in post-1990 in that deindustrialization has occurred.

Figure 3.7 illustrates the same comparison of the manufacturing shares of employment for the pre-1990 and the post-1990 period using the UNIDO dataset (i.e. formal manufacturing). Developing countries' employment shares have shifted from a strong upward pathway pre-1990 to a plateauing trend post-1990. The developing and former group too has experienced a shift; from a strongly rising curve to an outright inverted-U-shaped curve and premature deindustrialization post-1990.

Second, value-added shares: Figure 3.8 depicts the comparison of manufacturing value-added shares of the pre-1990 and the post-1990 period using the GGDC dataset (i.e. all manufacturing, formal and informal). Figure 3.9 illustrates the same using the UNSD dataset (i.e. formal manufacturing). The GGDC data shows more optimism for developing countries than the UNSD data. First, according to the GGDC data, the post-1990 period looks more optimistic for developing countries in value-added shares in the sense that the line is heading upwards rather than plateauing. The UNSD data show for both the developing countries group and the developing and former developing country grouping that the curves are past their peak in both periods with a lower peak post-1990. In sum, in terms of value-added shares, the post-1990 period is less worrisome for current developing countries in overall manufacturing and more worrying in formal manufacturing where the curve is heading downwards. Further, across all manufacturing value-added shares in developing countries are rising suggesting the informal sector is compensating for weaknesses of the formal sector to some extent. One important caveat: the datasets used have different end dates. The 10-Sector database covers the period to 2012; the INDSTAT-2 and National Accounts Main Aggregates database to 2017. Trends evident in the latter two datasets may thus not yet undiscernible in the former.

In sum, a set of stylized facts reads as follows. First, in terms of the thesis of premature deindustrialization we find that there is confirmation of that thesis in terms of a lower peak of employment shares for developing/former countries, and in the sense of a lower GDP per capita turning point. And although the premature deindustrialization thesis is not confirmed for value-added shares in all manufacturing, it is evident for value-added in formal manufacturing in the earlier turning point.

Further, the contemporary (post-1990) experience of current developing countries is—on average—of (i) plateauing employment shares in all manufacturing and in formal manufacturing or in other words, stalled industrialization but not, as far as the time the data covers, deindustrialization (yet); and (ii) falling value-added shares in formal manufacturing somewhat masked by rising shares in all manufacturing or in other words, stalled industrialization and early signs of deindustrialization of value-added in the formal sector amid growing shares in all manufacturing. It is worth noting that all of these stylized facts are by their nature an average trajectory for each group of countries. In other words, it is possible a small number of developing countries could buck the average trajectory.

Two questions arise from the above discussion: Does premature deindustrialization in employment shares; and in value-added in formal manufacturing matter? Does stalled industrialization matter in current developing countries matter? If so, why? In the next section it is argued that it does matter and furthermore, that the myth that economic development is sector-neutral is flawed.

3.4 The Second Myth of Economic Development

The myth accompanying the second transformation—the emergence of new varieties of structural transformation in the developing world—is that economic development is sector-neutral and thus, stalled industrialization and deindustrialization do not matter. In this section it is argued that this is not the case for developing countries. Theory and evidence to support this point comes from three sources. First, in terms of theory, classical theories of economic development consider manufacturing to be special and essential to economic development. This implies that stalled industrialization and deindustrialization are major problems for developing countries. Many theorists of the classical school, notably Kaldor (as well as numerous others) argued extensively that manufacturing is special. In the Lewis model, the modern sector—here formal manufacturing—is central in driving industrialization, economic growth, and job creation. Lewis (1979, p. 220) notes that:

> [T]he surest way to run into trouble is to have 'de-industrialization'…since this means that the reservoir of cheap labour will be filling instead of emptying. The political and social health of the community, no less its economic health, requires a continual transfer from the reservoir to the more productive sectors, rather than the relative expansion of the reservoir.

Pre-empting discussions of premature deindustrialisation, Kaldor developed in his detailed empirical investigation of the relationship between manufacturing and growth in the UK the concept of 'premature maturity'. This concept referred to an experience whereby manufacturing has 'exhausted its growth potential before attaining particularly high levels of productivity or average per capita income' (Kaldor, 1978 [1966], p. 102). He argued that early industrialization in the UK had exhausted the labour supply from agriculture too soon, or at least sooner than France or Germany and thus labour needed to transfer from services to manufacturing instead. Furthermore, industry wages in the UK were barely better than agriculture wages, so there was little reason for labour to move to manufacturing.

In short, in the classical school sectors matter as does activity specificity. Manufacturing is considered 'special' as it has increasing returns to scale (in direct contrast to the neoclassical theory of constant or decreasing returns to scale) and provides a host of spillovers. The neoclassical school is indifferent to sectors (in the Furtado/Lewisian sense) and specificity of economic activity (Herrendorf et al., 2015). The neo-classical school is represented by the Solow convergence models (traditional and augmented), endogenous models based on increasing returns, and models based on market imperfections in technological change. Although the importance of the shift to higher productivity is not disputed in neoclassical economics, a one-sector model of economic growth has become standard in macroeconomics (Herrendorf et al., 2015). This one-sector model of economic growth does not consider the process of inter-sectoral reallocation of economic activity or structural transformation. This is because in the neoclassical growth model (of Solow, 1956), growth is driven by incentives to save, accumulate physical and human capital, and innovate. The neoclassical position is that poorer countries will grow faster than rich countries and countries with the same technology will converge at a similar income level (see discussion in Sutirtha et al., 2016).

What binds the classical school group together intellectually is that growth dynamics are considered to be dependent on the sector and activities being developed, and on the capital accumulation effects of manufacturing in particular. Chenery (1975, 1979) and many others have argued that the sources of growth were not just capital accumulation, an increase in labour quantity and quality, increased intermediate inputs, and total factor productivity (TFP) as the neoclassical approach outlined, but also the reallocation of resources to higher productivity sectors, economies of scale, learning by doing, and the reduction of internal and external bottlenecks.

The classical school argues that issues such as technology, externalities, balance of payment sustainability, and convergence with advanced countries are a function of the size, strength, and depth of manufacturing. Manufacturing is *the* leading sector and a catalyst for economic development because of its ability to use technology, its increasing returns to scale, and also its tradability which removes the domestic market constraint of poor populations in developing countries. And herein lies the rub: As Rodrik (2016) argues most services are (i) non-tradeable and (ii) not technologically dynamic, and that (iii) some sectors are tradeable and dynamic, but they do not have the capacity to absorb labour.

In short, there is a core premise across the classical school that a structural imbalance in the sectoral distribution of production factors, which is not optimal for economic development may persist even in the long run. Baldwin and Forslid (2020, p. 27) sum up manufacturing's appeal in terms of economic development thus:

[A]number of well-known mechanisms...[have] made manufacturing-led development particularly attractive for developing-nation governments. First, rising manufacturing absorbed a lot of unskilled workers with minimal formal education, especially in unskilled-labor-intensive sectors such as clothing and footwear. They could, as it were, walk off the farm and into factories. In countries with growing masses of relatively uneducated young people and few jobs outside of subsistence agriculture, manufacturing was a blessing for social and political stability. Second, manufacturing activities were development 'escalators'. Marked by scale economies and technology spillovers, each extra manufacturing job was viewed as helping the nation and not just the individual worker.

Second, the detailed and extensive empirical historical study of Kaldor (1966, 1967) proves most forcefully that manufacturing was the engine of growth through the transfer of labour from low- to high-productivity sectors, the increasing returns to scale in manufacturing, and the higher output per person in manufacturing (versus agriculture and services). Kaldor argued that faster manufacturing growth would lead to faster labour transfer towards manufacturing, much like Lewis' analysis. Kaldor also argued that as labour moved towards manufacturing, the productivity of other sectors would rise too. In short, faster manufacturing growth would mean faster productivity growth overall. Kaldor (1968, p. 386) put it thus:

It is my contention that it is the rate at which this [labour] transfer takes place which determines the growth rate of productivity of the economy as a whole. The mechanism by which this happens is only to a minor extent dependent on the *absolute* differences in the levels of output per head between the labour-absorbing sectors and the surplus-labour sectors. The major part of the mechanism consists of the fact that the *growth* of productivity is accelerated as a result of the transfer at both ends – both at the gaining-end and the losing-end; in the first, because of increasing returns, productivity in industry will increase faster, the faster output expands; in the second, because when the surplus-sectors lose labour, the productivity of the remainder of the working population is bound to rise.

Kaldor (1966, 1967) sought to explain the economic development of Western Europe through the development of manufacturing, which he argued was the engine of growth for every country at every stage of economic development. He posited that economic development requires industrialization because increasing returns in the manufacturing sector mean faster growth of manufacturing output, which is associated with faster GDP growth. This is because backward and forward input–output linkages are strongest in manufacturing and the scope for capital accumulation, technological progress, economies of scale, and knowledge spillover is strong. There is a strong causal relationship between the growth of manufacturing output and labour productivity because of a deepening division of labour, specialization, and learning-by-doing. Moreover, the scope for productivity gains is large due to economies of scale.

Kaldor also noted that industrialization requires a basis in agricultural modernization to ensure food supply and that labour will transfer from other sectors to manufacturing. As manufacturing grows, productivity across the economy will rise overall—even in agriculture and services—through positive spillovers such as technological knowhow and complementary markets in services. Kaldor argued that the agriculture and industrial sectors are not only connected by the Lewis labour transition (the elastic supply of labour is due to industry wages exceeding agriculture wages) but also because agriculture creates autonomous demand for the manufacturing sector. Thus, land reform is required if agriculture is not to hinder structural transformation. Finally, as the economy grows, exports become increasingly important as a source of demand for the manufacturing sector. This is why Kaldor argued global competition requires temporary domestic industry protection accompanied by export-led growth policies.[6]

For Kaldor, the virtuous cycle is one of Myrdal's cycle of cumulative causation—that demand and output growth fuel productivity growth due to increasing returns to scale, which in turn fuels capital accumulation. Kaldor's (1966) interpretation of Verdoorn (1949) is that output growth induces improvements in labour productivity (assuming an elastic labour supply in

---

[6] Kaldor also took the two-sector model to be applicable to trade between developing and developed countries through the export of agriculture products from the former and import of manufactured goods from the latter. He argued that international trade could make developing countries poorer because liberalization would increase agriculture exports which are produced at decreasing returns that are not sufficient to compensate for the loss of manufacturing exports, which is a sector which produces increasing returns.

keeping with the Lewis model at the outset) and not vice versa. In contrast, the hypothesis of neoclassical models such as Solow is that productivity growth is due to technological progress. Verdoorn's argument was one of cumulative causation where demand rather than supply determines the rate of accumulation.

Third, in terms of the contemporary developing world and the cross-country *empirical* evidence, numerous studies have concurred that manufacturing is the lead sector and a driver of economic growth. For example, Szirmai and Verspagen (2015) consider 1950–2005 and 88 countries (of which 67 are developing countries) and find that the impact of manufacturing on growth was positive. Cantore et al. (2017) concur with a similar sample size. Pieper (2000) analysed a sample of 30 developing countries for 1975–84 and 1985–93 and found that industry contributed most to labour productivity in both periods. McMillan and Rodrik (2011), using 38 countries, conclude that the labour productivity differentials can be explained more by movements between sectors than by changes within sectors. This is not to say that within-sector labour movements to higher productivity tasks are unimportant. For example, Timmer and de Vries (2009) focus on 19 developing and developed countries for 1950–2005 and find that the within-sector effects were more important in *unweighted* average overall. Rather, the argument here is that movements of labour between sectors are essential to economic development and that this is empirically supported with reference to developing country samples.

Furthermore, McMillan and Rodrik (2011, p. 1), by considering sectoral and aggregate labour productivity data, show that the transfer of labour and other inputs to higher productive activity is a driver of economic development, as Lewis and others hypothesized. They, however, note that structural transformation can be growth-enhancing or growth-reducing, depending on the reallocation of labour. This is an important point and relates to the issue of movements of labour between sectors previously highlighted. McMillan and Rodrik show how structural change has been growth-enhancing in Asia because labour has transferred from low- to higher-productivity sectors. However, the converse is the case for sub-Saharan Africa and Latin America, where labour has transferred from higher- to lower-productivity sectors and consequently reduced growth rates.[7] Others, such as Herrendorf et al. (2013),

---

[7] McMillan and Rodrik (2011) find that countries with a large share of exports in natural resources tend to experience growth-reducing structural transformation and, even if they have higher productivity, cannot absorb surplus labour from agriculture. Gollin et al. (2016) also argued that natural resource exports drive urbanization without structural transformation because natural resources generate considerable surplus which is spent on urban goods and services, and urban employment tends to be in non-traded services. McMillan and Rodrik (2011) also find that an undervalued (competitive) exchange rate,

concur empirically with the argument that the sectoral composition of economic activity is key to understanding not only economic development but also productivity trends, business cycles, and wage inequality.

In sum, a body of theory and empirics supports the case that economic development is not sector-neutral. The body of theory is concerned with the Furtado/Lewisian movement of labour from 'traditional' or low-productivity activities/sectors to 'modern' or higher productivity activities/sectors, the relationship between sectors, and the 'special' role of manufacturing in driving economic development. These theories sit in contrast to the neoclassical model of economic growth, insofar that the neoclassical school is indifferent to Furtado/Lewis type sectors and the specificity of economic activity. This indifference is based on the assumption that an equilibrating process of marginal returns leads to an optimal allocation of production factors. However, the empirical evidence is strong that economic development is not sector-neutral and that in fact manufacturing is important for economic growth in developing countries. Empirical support for the relevance of the link between structural change and economic growth is abundant and countries that have raised income dramatically have done so through the process of industrialization (take for example, de Vries, Timmer, and de Vries, 2015; Duarte and Restuccia, 2010; Haraguchi et al., 2017; Herrendorf et al., 2013; McMillan et al., 2014; Rodrik, 2016; Szirmaiand Verspagen, 2015). Furthermore, a thriving manufacturing sector can lead to, as Hirschman (1958) argued the formation of backward and forward linkages which he argued drive economic development; as well as other positive externalities (Szirmai, 2012; Marconi et al., 2016) and to balance of payment sustainability (Cavalcanti et al., 2015). In other words, manufacturing has characteristics such as increasing returns to scale (in direct contrast to neoclassical theory of constant or decreasing returns to scale) and provides a host of spillovers (Chen, 2011; Storm, 2015; Szirmai and Verspagen, 2015; Pandian, 2017; Haraguchi et al., 2017; Cantore et al., 2017) that make manufacturing the preferable lead sector for economic development.

3.5 Conclusion

This chapter has explored the second great transformation since the Cold War. Namely, the shift in the form of economic development from industrialization

---

which operates effectively as a subsidy on industry and labour market characteristics (so that labour can easily move across sectors and firms), leads to growth-enhancing structural transformation.

towards stalled industrialization and deindustrialization. The accompanying myth of economic development as sector-neutral was critiqued. It was argued that stalled industrialization and deindustrialization in developing countries matter because of the 'special' role of manufacturing in economic development and employment creation in developing countries.

The chapter has presented a set of stylized facts based on empirical observation. First, that the traditional pathway of economic development—industrialization—is threatened by a new mode of stalled industrialization and deindustrialization. Second, that the thesis of premature deindustrialization of employment is confirmed for the developing/former countries in the sense of a lower shares and lower GDP per capita than developed countries achieved. Further, for value-added the premature deindustrialization thesis is not confirmed in all manufacturing, though it is confirmed for value-added in formal manufacturing. Third, the contemporary experience of current developing countries is one of a stalled industrialization in employment but not (yet) deindustrialization; and of a stalled industrialization with some indications of deindustrialization of value-added in the formal sector alongside growing shares in all manufacturing. We should not forget though that all of these stylized facts are average trajectories, meaning a small number of developing countries could break away from these patterns.

In the next two chapters, we discuss the impact of stalled industrialization and premature deindustrialization on economic growth in developing countries and on global inequality. More specifically, in Chapter 4 we focus on the impacts on the between-country component of global inequality, while in Chapter 5 we turn to the within-country component.

4

Income Inequality between Countries

Catch-up and Slow-down in a Value Chain World

4.1 Introduction

In Chapter 3, this book outlined the second great transformation since the Cold War affecting the world's two new middles of people and countries. In short, evidence of stalled industrialization and the threat of premature deindustrialization in developing countries. We argue in this chapter that the driver of this is a third great transformation since 1990. That third, system-wide global transformation—or structural evolution to echo Furtado's language—is the fragmentation of global production into a GVC world. In a GVC world, production is dispersed across countries and production is orchestrated—though not necessarily with the ownership of production—by TNCs. This transformation has in some ways strengthened the early possibilities for economic development for low-income developing countries, some argue. At the same time this transformation has weakened the prospects for sustaining economic development rapidly beyond middle-income. Furthermore, peripherality and to some extent a new form of dependency have evolved, whereby developing countries have become suppliers to GVCs, dependent on GVC access for economic development whilst developed countries remain home to the higher-value-added activities of the chains and the TNCs that orchestrate the chains. The myth accompanying this third great transformation is that if developing countries integrate more and more into GVC world, they will drive and sustain economic development in the longer term.

The third transformation matters in particular to the first new middle of countries—middle-income developing countries—because it will determine their future growth prospects to some considerable extent. Indeed, stalled industrialization and premature deindustrialization impact the between-country component of global inequality through their influence on future economic growth in middle-income developing countries.

In this chapter, we connect the processes of stalled industrialization, premature deindustrialization, and accompanying tertiarization with the

Deindustrialization, Distribution, and Development: Structural Change in the Global South. Andy Sumner, Oxford University Press.
© Andrew Sumner 2021. DOI: 10.1093/oso/9780198853008.003.0004

implications for the new middle of countries, MICs, and the between-country component of global inequality. In Chapter 5, we connect the same processes of stalled industrialization, premature deindustrialization, tertiarization, and the emergence of a GVC world with the within-country component of global inequality. We argue in this chapter that stalled industrialization and premature deindustrialization in the developing world are driven by the changes in global production emerging since the end of the Cold War. In particular, they are driven by the fragmentation of global manufacturing into a GVC world and the resulting diminishing of economic development to a form of shallow and stunted development. This means economic development is fuelled for a while and then economic opportunities diminish around middle-income levels. It is important to note that this is *not* the same as arguing that developing countries have never benefited from GVC participation. The presentation of this book is that—*on average*—developing countries may benefit for a while as they integrate into GVCs but then benefits diminish and may even turn negative as productivity rises. As a consequence, economic development—even the shallow progress—may not be sustained. The idea that if developing countries integrate more and more into GVC world, this will on average drive and sustain economic development in the long term is the myth accompanying the third transformation. In this chapter, we argue that the GVC-driven model of economic development leads, at best, to a shallow and stunted form of economic development and that the benefits of GVC participation diminish at the productivity levels achieved in most middle-income countries and then may turn negative.

In other words, economic development driven by GVC integration dictates parameters on what is achievable for developing countries. Some developing countries may achieve some economic development, at least up to a point, and then stagnate at middle-income levels, with few countries attaining structural characteristics of advanced countries. In fact, Felipe et al. (2018) find that it is very rare to grow into a high-income country (HIC) (defined as US$12,000 GDP per capita in 2005 prices during 2005–10) without first developing a large manufacturing sector.[1] They find that employment in manufacturing is a good predictor of future high-income status. They find that all current HICs achieved manufacturing employment shares above 18 per cent at some point since the 1970s. The maximum employment share for a typical MIC today is just 13 to 15 per cent, which suggests that the achievement of HIC status will be less likely for today's MICs. In other words,

---

[1] Felipe et al. (2018) find a positive and statistically significant relationship between per capita income in 2005–10 and the historical peak shares of manufacturing employment (and to some lesser extent manufacturing output).

the peak of manufacturing employment and to a lesser extent manufacturing value-added is an important determinant of eventual prosperity.

In Chapter 3, based on the classical school's theories of economic development, we discussed why stalled industrialization and premature deindustrialization matter for developing countries. We examined the 'special' developmental characteristics of manufacturing. Now, in this chapter, we pick up the discussion and turn to the drivers and the consequences of stalled industrialization and premature deindustrialization. We first focus on the impacts of changes in global manufacturing since the Cold War and the emergence of a GVC world on developing countries' prospects. We assess the empirical evidence and subsequently develop theory to explain the persistence of the between-country component of global inequality.

This chapter is structured as follows: Section 4.2 considers the third transformation, specifically, the fragmentation of global production and the impacts of changes in global manufacturing on developing countries. Section 4.3 considers the empirical evidence on GVC integration, and productivity and employment growth. Section 4.4 then develops theory to explain the relationship between GVC world, stalled industrialization and premature deindustrialization and global inequality. Section 4.5 concludes.

4.2 The Emergence of a GVC World

In this section, it is argued that stalled industrialization and premature deindustrialization are primarily driven by the dynamics of late development in a GVC world. That GVC world is a world where global manufacturing is spread thinner and thinner across more and more countries due to the ongoing fragmentation of global production. The emergence of a GVC world has simultaneously generated new dynamics of *centrifugal forces*—referring to the dispersal of economic activities—and, conversely, of *centripetal forces*—which is the functional integration of companies and industries regardless of political borders. The process of fragmentation involves what Baldwin and Venables (2013) call 'snakes' and 'spiders' as well as mixtures of these. A GVC 'snake' is a production process whereby intermediate goods are sent from one country to another to be incorporated into intermediate goods that go on to another country. In contrast, in the case of a GVC 'spider', multiple intermediate parts come together from various locations to a single assembly place.

In keeping with this, Dean et al. (2007, p. 1) refer to the new GVC world overall as follows:

[P]roduction processes are sliced thinner and thinner into many stages, and the resulting production fragments are carried out in different locations. The production of a finished product thus involves the participation of many economies, with countries specializing in different fragments of the vertical production chain.... While the international division of labour in the global economy is nothing new, the vast scope and the intricate nature of this pattern of global production sharing seems genuinely unprecedented.

That said, the fragmentation of GVCs is characteristic of manufacturing GVCs rather than resource-based sectors. Kaplinsky and Morris (2016) differentiate between these two types of GVCs. First, there are vertically specialized GVCs such as those Dean et al. point towards. Second, there are additive GVCs. The first, for Kaplinsky and Morris, vertically specialized GVCs, are a result of lead firms' focus on core activities and out-sourcing of non-core activities leading to fragmentation of the production into a set of sub-processes. This lends itself to global dispersion because there is no need for stages to be co-located. In general, manufacturing illustrates well this kind of GVC. The second, additive GVCs, in contrast, entail the sequential adding of value at each stage. These kind of GVCs characterize resource sectors. These are relatively immobile, as they require resource extraction. In this book, the focus is on the former given the discussion is about manufacturing in particular.

Focusing on the fragmentation of manufacturing in particular, Baldwin (2006, 2016, 2019, 2020a, 2020b) talks of processes of 'unbundling'—a geographic separation of production and consumption in the first instance—driven by arbitrage or differences in relative prices across countries (so it is possible to buy-low and sell-high). The first 'unbundling'—the unbundling of production and consumption—in the global economy occurred in the 1850–1914 period and further from the 1960s onwards, resulting in the geographic separation of production and consumption. This, Baldwin argues, was followed by a further second unbundling from the mid-1980s onwards—an unbundling of factories—in the form of production fragmentation via offshoring and outsourcing, driven by liberalization and digitalization. This unbundling was crucial to the creation of a GVC world and for Baldwin and Okubo (2019) 'denationalized' comparative advantage from nations to GVCs. In this unbundling, echoing Furtado, 'the G7 firms retain control of [the firms] technology as they apply it to labour in non-G7 nations and the resulting cost reduction boost the G7 firm's competitiveness' (Baldwin and Okubo, 2019, p. 54). The ICT revolution—where firms can monitor factories in real time and at low cost—drove offshoring and fragmentation. This led to the share of G7 countries in global manufacturing to fall from about two-thirds in 1990 to less than half in 2010 and a sixth of the world's manufacturing moved from outside China to inside China (Baldwin and Okubo, 2019, p. 55). Looking ahead, Baldwin (2019, 2020a, 2020b) argues, the next unbundling is coming or in process; namely, the expansion of tradable services due to digitalization and the potential for some services to be undertaken by 'tele-migrating' or working online, thus moving jobs from OECD countries with higher labour costs to developing countries with lower labour costs.

The establishment of a GVC world was a policy (i.e. political) choice—though perhaps not fully anticipated by those making those choices—in the form of enactment of economic liberalization policies that made the fragmentation of production and the very existence of GVCs possible. The emergence of a GVC world has been further accelerated by technological advances noted and industry-level standards that allow for complicated information transfers to be made to and from each of the links in the chain using supply chain software and the tagging of components. In short, new technology and GVCs are interwoven in such a way as to make the GVC-participating sectors akin to Lewis' modern or Furtado's nucleus sector. Furtado (2020 [1974], p. 20) himself noted how 'the large company controls innovation within national economies... [via] the introduction of new process and new products'. For Furtado, this labour-saving technical change from richer countries was a driver of stagnation, as it was not appropriate to the labour abundance in developing countries. More recently, Rodrik (2018, p. 3) puts it thus with reference to GVCs:

> The introduction of these new technologies in production in developing countries often takes place through global value chains (GVCs). GVCs are in effect part and parcel of the new technology. Improvements in communication and information technologies have enabled large firms based in advanced nations, whether retailers or manufacturers, to divide the production chain into specific tasks that can then be dispersed around the globe to take advantage of lower costs. GVCs in turn serve as the vehicle for the dissemination of technology from the lead firms to their suppliers.

Selwyn (2012) traces a genealogy of the analysis of GVCs to radical roots in world-systems theory's commodity chain approach some fifty years ago. World-systems theory introduced the concept of a hierarchy of periphery, semi-periphery and core in the global economy. Wallerstein (1979) developed the concept of 'semi-peripheralism' and Arrighi (1990) argued that the semi-periphery only gains when it trades with the periphery (not the core). Emmanuel (1972) placed the mobility of capital as the driver for rising global inequality between countries, arguing that the size of the core's surplus value will increase as the size of the periphery's surplus value falls. In sum, capital mobility—or as we see in GVCs *virtual mobility* in the sense that factories do not physically move but rather who is chosen as the supplier leads to value transfer from the periphery to the core, as it changes the terms of trade— could hinder long-term economic development in the periphery.

As Selwyn (2012) notes, Gereffi (1994) reformulated the GVC-analytic from critical theory to a problem-solving theory, outlining the global restructuring and institutional questions arising. Much research on GVCs has focused on labour-intensive manufacturing. However, following on from the demarcation made by Kaplinsky and Morris (2016), GVCs are also widespread in resources sectors and also modern agro-food and, as Baldwin points out, increasingly too in modern tradable services, such as business and financial services including call centres and information processing services. Furthermore, the oft-used economic sector boundaries have blurred somewhat and within manufacturing, some firms may provide intermediate tasks—services—that feed into other GVCs. Felipe et al. (2014, p. 5, n. 3) sum it up thus:

> Many manufacturing companies are outsourcing non-core operation (e.g. marketing, warehousing, transport, information technology) and many manufactured products are increasingly bundled with a host of services (e.g. after-sales services, such as extended warranties, repair services, telephone helplines). This has been a process where manufacturing firms have shed many of their services functions to increase efficiency.

In short, the complexity of a GVC world means we face a data 'snag' as Kaldor (1961) put it, that a perfect separation of manufacturing and non-manufacturing in the data is not plausible. That said, such trends—the fuzziness of sectors—are not driving deindustrialization as far as the country level data tell us (see the detailed empirical study of Nayyar et al., 2018).

As noted in the earlier chapters, the emergence of a GVC world has changed the very meaning of economic development from 'deep' industrialization to 'shallow' industrialization in the sense that the building of entire industries or even entire products is no longer even the goal for developing countries. Furthermore, the emergence of a GVC world has changed the nature of economic development from one of potentially unbounded industrialization to stunted industrialization. This is because—as we discuss empirically in the following section—participation in GVCs may initially boost productivity and employment but will, in the long-run, lead to a stunted economic development when productivity reaches middle-income levels because the benefits diminish and may turn negative as productivity rises. Moreover, if lead TNCs switch suppliers for commercial reasons, it leaves behind hollowed out and stalling industrialization processes or even deindustrialization. The holy grail thus becomes 'economic upgrading', meaning a movement towards high-value-added activities in the same GVC or another GVC through better technology, skills training, and knowledge development.[2] Upgrading is not easy though because one major factor determining upgrading is that the lead TNCs of the GVCs operate in oligopolistic markets with entry barriers in the form of patents, trademarks, and standards (what Kaldor called 'institutional monopolies') and/or TNCs squeeze suppliers to reduce prices. In short, lead firms can enable or constrain domestic firms' scope for upgrading to some considerable extent (see discussion in Humphrey and Schmitz, 2002).

GVCs have thus transformed the economic development options available to developing countries. Instead of pursuing deep economic development by building industries (as per import-substitution industrialization strategies), domestic companies in developing countries—with reference to manufacturing—become suppliers for specific parts of a product built across many countries that are joined together into a production process led by TNCs in oligopolistic global markets.

In spite of these limitations, the pursuit of export-led growth via GVCs has been very much promoted by international agencies to address weak industrialization in developing countries. Somewhere in between the optimistic (economic development is 'easier' for developing countries) and pessimistic perspectives (developing countries are, at best, in the lower-value-added activities in the mid-range of the 'smile curve') noted in the introductory chapter is that GVC participation is a 'mixed blessing' thesis (of Pahl and Timmer, 2020). This means that GVCs engender an initial boost to employment and productivity, though make industrialization less meaningful as capabilities may not be built. Specifically, following Rodrik (2018), the technologies inherent within GVCs provide less opportunities for unskilled labour and may require higher levels of automation (due to, for example,

---

[2] Building on Humphrey and Schmitz (2002), Barrientos et al. (2011) propose four forms of economic upgrading: process upgrading or changes in the productive process to be more efficient (i.e. automation); product upgrading or the development of more advanced product types which means more skilled jobs; chain upgrading or moving to a more technologically sophisticated GVC; and functional upgrading whereby attempts are made to move towards the end and the beginning of the GVCs to perform, for example, branding and design or logistics and transportation.

adhering to the precision of quality standards) echoing Furtado's worries about technology imported from advanced countries. In spite of promoting GVC participation, the World Bank (2020) concurred that the biggest growth spurt occurs when entering manufacturing GVCs from commodity GVCs and that there are diminishing and even negative returns if developing countries stay in this 'entry' phase of manufacturing GVCs. In other words, the relationship between economic development—structural transformation, productivity growth, and employment growth—and GVC integration is not linear, as the benefits from GVC integration may decline over time and may even turn negative. The benefit of joining GVCs is larger for lower-income countries, then shrinks for middle-income countries, and expands again for high-income countries as they take advantage of low-income countries in GVCs or because they are home to leading TNCs who make use of their dominant position and oligopolistic market power. If developing countries fail to upgrade domestic production structures after extracting the initial benefits of joining a GVC, then they could become stuck in a 'GVC trap' or in the middle of Shih's 'smile curve' and initial economic growth and employment generation may not be sustained.

What is empirically known about the impacts of changes in global production on middle-income developing countries? The body of cross-country, quantitative research on GVC integration and economic development is rather mixed in terms of samples, approaches, and findings. Some studies consider developing or developed countries only, whereas others look at both. Some are focused on specific countries or industries and use macroeconomic indicators as their variables of interest. Other studies go as far as to make international comparisons with the analysis of different ways of participating in GVCs. In general, two points are worth noting about this body of quantitative research. First, most studies suffer from a limited sample and an unbalanced panel. As a result, the conclusions drawn are tentative and thus open to question. It is contentious to use an unbalanced panel and limited or very short time-series data to conduct a cause–effect evaluation in a regression analysis. Furthermore, some studies use data from Organisation for Economic Co-operation and Development (OECD) countries only (e.g. Agostino et al., 2015; Hogrefe and Yao, 2016; Budd et al., 2005). Hence, their relevance to middle-income developing countries is questionable, given that GVC lead firms are primarily based in OECD countries and since OECD countries have different structural characteristics to middle-income developing countries. In contrast, other studies use data from both OECD and developing countries (e.g. Kowalski et al., 2015; Kummritz et al., 2017). While these studies do not report results for each country group separately they do show nuance. For example, Kummritz et al. (2017), using a dataset of 61 countries and 34 industries over the period 1995–2011, find that the consequences of GVC participation depend on the level of income of a country, the type of GVC integration (buyer or seller), transmission channels such as backward and forward linkages to local firms, and the demand for skilled labour. Their results are that being a seller—i.e. forward linkages in GVCs—contributes more clearly to upgrading than being a buyer—i.e. backward linkages in GVCs. Some studies do have a developing country focus, but they have such small samples that the generalizability of their findings is very much open to contention (e.g. Morrison et al., 2008; Pietrobelli and Rabellotti, 2011). Pahl and Timmer (2020) are the notable exception, which is why we discuss their study in more depth below.

Second, studies tend to find that GVC integration can lead to economic downgrading as well as upgrading. Some studies conducted at both firm- and country-level tend to show more positive outcomes for developing countries (Benkovskis et al., 2017; Bernhardt and Pollak, 2016; Del Prete et al., 2017; Díaz-Mora et al., 2018; Giuliani et al., 2005; Hijzen et al., 2013; Ivarsson and Alvstam, 2011). However, other studies of developing countries find that GVC integration does not lead to upgrading or even leads to downgrading (e.g. Gimet et al., 2015; Milberg and Winkler, 2011).

In general, the studies lean towards the idea that the outcomes from GVC integration differ across countries. Some countries experienced a positive impact on employment, whereas in other countries GVC integration had no impact or even a negative influence on wages, employment, or both (Banga, 2016; Gimet et al., 2015; Pahl and Timmer, 2020). Furthermore, benefits are conditional upon contextual factors, such as different regimes of capitalism and industrial policies in particular, the use of state-owned enterprises as well as the domestic policy environment; the maturity of the participating firms; and the geographic location and proximity of developing countries to the leading firms and sectors (see, for discussion, Barrientos et al., 2016; Gereffi, 2018).

As useful as these studies are, the current body of quantitative studies in this area has rarely grappled with bigger questions about global inequality or stalled industrialization and premature deindustrialization. One important issue is that of measurement. In general, there are two approaches to measuring GVC participation. The first takes firm-level or product-level survey data. Examples include studies of Apple's supply chain and China (e.g. Linden et al., 2009; Dedrick et al., 2010). In this approach, the components of a product are attributed to the countries that made them. This approach is firm- or product-based and thus does not seek to understand the systematic role of GVCs in a country.

In contrast, a different approach to measuring GVC participation is to use input–output tables and the import content of exports (first developed by Hummels et al., 2001 and used by studies mentioned above such as Kummritz et al., 2017).[3] For example, Koopman et al. (2014) developed a framework for decomposing gross exports into exported value-added, returning domestic value-added as well as foreign value-added and other items.

At a basic level, there are major limitations in the coverage of datasets for developing countries. The oft-used Trade in Value-Added (TIVA) database of the OECD (2018) currently only covers 14 developing plus three former developing economies (Korea, Singapore, Taiwan) for 1995–2016, meaning that samples in many of the studies discussed may be skewed by the large proportion of advanced economies in the sample. Many of the latter are also home to lead firms in GVCs and thus more likely to benefit from higher-value-added benefits from the value chain as noted. In addition to the OECD TiVA database, UNCTAD collates the UNCTAD-Eora GVC database (see Casella et al., 2019) which has data for 189 countries for 1990–2018 but it includes countries that do not produce input-output tables. Data is generated from EORA Multi-Region Input-Output tables. Importantly, there is also the high-quality, novel dataset of Pahl and Timmer (2020) which covers almost 40 developing countries which we use later in this chapter (see later discussion).

If we turn next to the qualitative research in the area, Coe and Yeung's (2019) review provides a useful summary. In general qualitative studies have been more critical in nature (e.g. Barrientos et al., 2016; Kaplinsky, 2000). The Coe and Yeung review emphasizes the focus on the shifting patterns of uneven development in the capitalist world economy, labour right abuses, and asymmetrical power relations between TNCs and suppliers in developing countries. They note a bias towards the 'dark side' of GVCs which they refer to as 'disarticulation perspectives' (see Yeung, 2015, 2016). For example, Mosley (2017), Blair (2017), and Posthuma and Rossi (2017) show rising wages and improved job opportunities in some places and sectors but not in others. Other scholars have made connections between the workings of a GVC world and the dynamics of poverty and inequality (e.g. Phillips, 2017; Kaplinsky, 2014) by analysing the mechanisms of labour and labour exploitation; market, social, and political asymmetries; the concentration of

---

[3] Timmer et al. (2014) and others have used such an approach at international level to capture inter-country and inter-industry links.

market power and the generation of rents; and how barriers are erected to entry to, and participation in, GVCs (for both countries and producers). One important finding of qualitative research is that inequalities arising from labour exploitation are especially pronounced in the most price-sensitive and labour-intensive sectors (Fransen and Burgoon, 2012; Knorringa, 2014; Phillips, 2017).

In sum, the study of the developmental impact of GVC participation is well established. That said, in substantive terms, insufficient attention has been given to date to studies of GVC participation that explore the 'big picture' or the relationship between the emergence of a GVC world and the persistence of global inequality. In fact, the biggest weaknesses of GVC research are the dominance of firm-centric analysis which conceals the role of the state, labour, and politics (see Phelps et al., 2018; Werner, 2016, 2018); the lack of attention to the big questions about global inequality and how the success of some regions may come at the expense of others (see Coe and Yeung, 2019) and the focus on micro-development at the expense of macro-development (see McGrath, 2018).

In methodological terms, the current measurement of GVC participation has often led past studies to take a reductive approach to assessing GVC integration by inferring that all GVC integration is the same. Consequently, studies may fail to account for how becoming 'stuck' at certain GVC access points impacts a country's developmental outcomes. This means that a country's stage of development at the time of its integration into GVCs as well as its positioning within the value chain itself can determine whether GVC integration will be positive or not. At an earlier stage in a country's development, even joining the lower end of the value chain could stimulate economic development, as integration into GVCs could cause a movement of labour from the traditional, low-productivity sector to the modern, higher-productivity sectors. However, this benefit will erode over time as the overall productivity of that country increases. As such, countries which have been successful in economic development, such as China, may over time seek to even reduce GVC participation in terms of the foreign proportion of exports. China, for example, has seen the foreign proportion of gross exports fall dramatically (from 38 per cent in 2004 to 17 per cent in 2016) (OECD, 2018). This undoubtedly raises the question as to whether the desirable direction of GVC integration is to increase the import share of value-added in exports or whether this is 'value-added erosion' (Caraballo and Jiang, 2016). In the following section we consider the empirics of GVC participation with a focus on developing countries and on different kinds of sectors by technology.

4.3 The Empirics of GVC Integration

In terms of the empirical association, many studies noted in the earlier discussion suffer from samples which include only few developing countries. One detailed study that has rectified this weakness is that of Pahl and Timmer (2020), who explore the impact of GVC participation on productivity and employment in manufacturing in almost 40 developing countries and 20 HICs over the period 1970–2008. They apply a Lewisian lens and focus on manufacturing activities that are integrated into a GVC world make use of the UNIDO INDSTAT-2 dataset and thus formal manufacturing. Pahl and Timmer's aim is to assess whether a country's participation in GVCs is associated with productivity and employment growth in the formal (modern) manufacturing sector. They compile a new long-run dataset of input–output tables in the vein of Chenery et al. (1986) for 1970–2008 and find support for the 'mixed blessing' hypothesis. They make use of novel measures of domestic value-added and employment generated by exporting. Pahl and Timmer measure all manufacturing value-added and employment activity generated in exports and also related, upstream industries, hence not just the industry of firms that export.[4] They find strong evidence of the positive impacts of GVC participation on productivity growth in formal manufacturing and the effect is stronger further from the productivity frontier, i.e. the poorest countries entering GVCs. However, surprisingly they find no evidence for a positive impact on employment generation, concurring with Formai and Vergara Caffarelli (2016) who study 50 countries in the 1990s and 2000s. Pahl and Timmer find no evidence for a positive impact on employment generation even if conditioning for other determinants or using five or ten year periods. The employment effects even turn negative at middle-income productivity levels, they note. The findings hold for sub-sets of countries and industries. There is no positive association with employment growth even in the countries of East and South-East Asia, which are found to have the strongest productivity gains from GVC participation. That said, as they note, the findings are on average and some countries—they highlight China and Thailand—have achieved productivity and employment gains through GVC participation. Furthermore, Timmer et al. (2014) estimate the number of new jobs created by GVC participation in manufacturing to be 40 million in China. Pahl and Timmer hypothesize their employment

---

[4] Pahl and Timmer make use of the Los et al. (2016) GVC participation index. In the GVC index, a value closer to 1 shows manufacturing to have a higher level of GVC integration, meaning exports are more reliant on input intermediates. A value close to 0 shows the opposite. The Pahl and Timmer dataset is available online.

findings stem from an unskilled labour bias in modern technologies that is diffused through modern manufacturing firms who participate in GVCs. They further highlight that employment growth turns significantly negative at productivity levels that are characteristic of middle-income countries. Pahl and Timmer conclude that on average, GVC participation is indeed a mixed blessing for the long-term development of poor countries, though this finding does not preclude the possibility that GVC participation has been growth-enhancing for some countries in particular periods. It does though point to the fact that there are many cases in which GVC participation may have engendered a modern sector expansion with little job creation.

We next utilise, with grateful thanks, the dataset of Pahl and Timmer's study and we construct a set of figures (see Figures 4.1 and 4.2). The figures show the marginal effects of changes in the GVC participation index by different levels of initial labour productivity in manufacturing exports overall; and by the level of technological intensity of manufacturing sub-sectors.

Not surprisingly as we are using their dataset, we corroborate the Pahl and Timmer conclusions in a sense that GVC participation is a 'mixed blessing' because there are initial gains in labour productivity for those developing countries at low levels of labour productivity and there is a surprisingly weak effect of GVC participation on employment growth.

What does the data say? Again, it is possible to make a set of empirical observations or stylized facts. Figure 4.1 (left-hand side) shows the marginal effects of changes in the GVC participation index on labour productivity

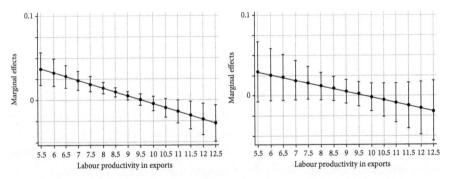

Figure 4.1 Marginal effects of GVC participation on labour productivity growth (left-hand side) and employment growth (right-hand side), in developing countries by levels of labour productivity in exports, 1970–2008.

Note: Figure shows the marginal effects of changes in the GVC participation index by different levels of initial labour productivity in exports; vertical lines are confidence intervals; sample of 37 developing countries (1152 observations); countries classified as developing countries (LIC, LMIC or UMIC) in 1990.

Source: Author based on Pahl and Timmer (2020) dataset which is drawn from UNIDO INDSTAT-2 dataset and Pahl and Timmer (2019).

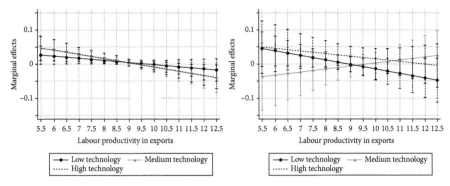

Figure 4.2 Marginal effects of GVC participation on labour productivity growth (left-hand side) and employment growth (right-hand side), in developing countries by levels of labour productivity in exports and sub-sector technological intensity, 1970–2008.

Note: Figure shows the marginal effects of changes in the GVC participation index by different levels of initial labour productivity in exports in different sub-sectors of manufacturing grouped by technology intensity; vertical lines are confidence intervals; sample of 37 developing countries (and 534, 261, 357 observations for low technology, medium technology and high technology manufacturing sub-sectors, respectively). Countries classified as developing countries (LIC, LMIC or UMIC) in 1990.

Source: Author based on Pahl and Timmer (2020) dataset which is drawn from UNIDO INDSTAT-2 dataset and Pahl and Timmer (2019).

growth in manufacturing exports. Labour productivity is measured by dividing the nominal value-added by employment, drawing on Rodrik (2013). The figure shows the mean marginal effect at each level of productivity. The figure shows the effect of GVC participation for developing countries is positive at lower levels labour productivity.

Figure 4.1 illustrates that the effect of GVC participation on labour productivity growth is stronger for developing countries that are further from the productivity frontier. In short, very poor countries (lowest productivity) on average make labour productivity gains from GVC participation. However, this effect diminishes as levels of productivity rise and turns negative at productivity levels associated with middle-income countries.

Figure 4.1 (right-hand side) shows the marginal effects of GVC participation on employment growth. In developing countries, the employment effects are—on average—minimal in very poor countries (lowest productivity) and actually turn negative around productivity levels associated with MICs. The marginal effects of GVC participation on employment growth in developing countries are consistent with a labour–capital substitution effect that results from the use of modern technology in GVCs.

Next we consider the marginal effects of GVC participation on productivity and employment growth in manufacturing *sub-sectors* grouped by technology intensity. We group sub-sectors by the UNIDO's (2010, 2020) typology of sub-sectors in manufacturing. The UNIDO classification is derived from research and development (R&D) expenditure incurred in manufacturing goods production. High technology industries have higher R&D intensity (measured as the ratio of R&D expenditure to gross value-added) and vice versa, low technology industries have lower R&D intensity.[5]

Figure 4.2 shows the results. A caveat is very important. The number of observations is relatively low in some of the sub-sectors (see notes under figures) thus these results should be viewed as exploratory. With that in mind, what does the data say? First, we can say that the labour productivity gains for developing countries from more GVC participation are—not surprisingly—weaker in low technology sub-sectors—i.e. more labour-intensive industries (e.g. textiles)—than medium or higher technology sub-sectors. This is of note because the low technology sub-sectors is where most developing countries are likely to enter GVCs. Second, for developing countries the employment gains from more GVC participation are—again not surprisingly—clearer in low technology sectors (i.e. more labour intensive). This is of note because many of these employment opportunities may be a historical fact that is shifting over time due to technical change (see Chapter 5). In short, the data point to a productivity vs employment trade-off overall for developing countries in low technology sub-sectors. Further, the employment gains for developing countries—on average—diminish as productivity levels rise and turn negative much earlier than in high technology sub-sectors. Also, medium technology sub-sectors are initially negative in terms of employment gains but do turn positive as low technology sectors turn negative, though weakly. This suggests that those countries that do upgrade from low to medium technology GVCs may see—on average—some minimal employment gains. It is necessary here to reiterate: the number of observations is *relatively low* in some of the sub-sectors. Furthermore, the data is (inevitably) historical data and technical change may mean different future patterns; and the dataset runs only to 2008.

---

[5] In Figure 4.2 low technology sub-sectors (and ISIC Rev 3.29 codes) refer to food (15, 16); textiles and wearing apparel (17, 18); leather, leather products and footwear (19); wood products excluding furniture (20); and paper products, printing, and publishing (21, 22). Medium technology sub-sectors refer to rubber and plastic products (25), non-metallic mineral products (26), and basic metals and fabricated metal products (27, 28). High technology sub-sectors are chemicals and chemical products (24); machinery and equipment (29); office, accounting, and computing machinery; electronic machinery and apparatus; radio, TV, and communication equipment; medical, precision, and optical instruments (30–3); and motor vehicles, trailers, semi-trailers, and other transport equipment (34, 35). See also discussion in Galindo-Rueda and Verger (2016). In contrast, Pahl and Timmer divide sectors by type of GVCs. Specifically, GVCs using relatively sophisticated intermediates (machinery, electronics, transport equipment), GVCs using relatively less sophisticated intermediates (food, textiles, leather, wood, paper and printing, and manufacturing not elsewhere classified), and resource-intensive GVCs (chemicals, rubber, non-metallic minerals, and metals). In short, in the figures the classifications are similar though the terms are different.

In sum, in addition to the well-known smile curve, one could plot a non-linear, inverted-U or what one could call a 'frown curve' which represents the relationship between increasing GVC participation for developing countries and the economic development of developing countries. For developing countries, this curve is as important as the oft-cited 'smile curve'. The 'frown curve' if drawn would show an inverted-U curve with the initial benefits from GVC participation for low-productivity economies, and benefits diminish as productivity rises and turn negative around middle-income levels. In short, the benefit of joining GVCs are clearer for lower-income countries, then shrink for middle-income countries and may even turn negative.

4.4 Beyond the Third Myth of Economic Development

The myth accompanying the third great transformation is that if developing countries integrate more and more into GVC world, the process of integration will drive and sustain economic development in the long run. This is not likely to be the case as is evident from the empirical discussion of the previous section. This section instead develops theory to explain the relationship between a GVC world, stalled industrialization and premature deindustrialization in the developing world, and the between-country component of global inequality.

In this section, it is argued that in order to understand stalled industrialization and deindustrialization, it is necessary to build on the discussion in earlier chapters relating to late development and the role of manufacturing as the lead sector or special sector in late economic development. This is crucial in order to integrate an understanding of late economic development with the dualism of Furtado and Lewis in the contemporary period of global economic history.

We next discuss here how deindustrialization, the emergence of a GVC world, and global inequality are connected. There are four components to a theory explaining the causal connections and the persistence of global inequality. First, the dynamics of the new global system. Second, the situation of developing countries in the new global system. Third, the dualism of Furtado and Lewis that can explain the contemporary economic development in terms of sectoral movements. Finally, the 'energy' driving the system, which is intense competition between numerous middle-income developing countries (and increasingly some LICs too) that have a relatively small number of internationally competitive firms each.

First, the dynamics of a GVC world. A recap: We can characterize a GVC world post-1990 in contrast to what could be called a pre-GVC world pre-1990 (value chains were more regional and, in some cases, national). Post-1990, the global production of manufactured goods is fragmented across numerous countries. The higher-valued activities at the beginning (e.g. design) and the end of the chain (e.g. marketing) are typically conducted in OECD countries. Lead TNCs in each GVC orchestrate the process and, as noted, are usually based in OECD countries rather than developing countries with a relatively small number of exceptions of Southern TNCs.

Second, we can situate developing countries within this new global system. Developing countries compete to 'capture' a piece of the global manufacturing process to stimulate their own national economic development. The benefits of GVC participation follow an inverted-U shape in that the benefits initially accrue and assist low-income countries up to a point but decline over time, especially if a country becomes stuck at a lower-productivity GVC access point. The decline comes in the form of weaker economic growth and employment creation as a result of continued GVC participation.

Third, the dualism of Furtado and Lewis is useful to explain the economic development of developing countries in the new global system. One could think of the two-sector model and superimpose on the traditional sector the label 'non-GVC sector' and on the modern sector the label 'GVC sector'. The former is synonymous with lower levels of productivity vis-à-vis the latter. Labour transfers initially from the non-GVC sector to the modern, GVC sector. The driver of capital accumulation is the sectoral movement of labour from the 'traditional'/non-GVC sector to the modern/GVC sector of higher productivity (where wages are set by productivity in the non-GVC sector) and where modern technology is used as production is 'fructified' by capital as Lewis (1954) put it.

If the GVC/modern sector is expanding, productivity and employment growth occur as labour is pulled into the GVC/modern sector. If suppliers to GVCs lose contracts and the GVC/modern sector stops expanding, workers face a choice to move to a bifurcated traditional sector of informal, low-productivity services in urban areas or to informal, non-GVC manufacturing. Lewis (1958) actually refers to the latter as the 'in-between sector' which may have lower wages, lower productivity, and act as a 'sponge' sector absorbing workers, at least temporarily. For Lewis, the 'in-between sector' of informal manufacturing is *domestic-orientated* manufacturing. As he put it:

An economy does not divide into a capitalist sector hiring workers for factories and other large units on the one hand, and a small farming sector on the other hand. In between are units of production of all sizes, and in particular, a great number of one-to-five-man undertakings in manufacturing, transport and a wide range of services – often nowadays called the informal sector. Some of this activity belongs in the modern sector as we have defined it, i.e. it will expand with economic development; the rest – e.g. some of the handicrafts and some of the services – belong to the traditional sector in that they will contract. The expansion of small scale activity in the modern sector is an important part of the development process…because this sector of the economy is useful in its own right, meeting genuine market needs, and providing a lot of employment in the process.

(Lewis, 1958, p. 222)

In keeping with this, Diao and McMillan (2018) develop a three-sector Lewisian model to incorporate an 'in-between' sector or in fact, a *dualism within dualism*, meaning a dualism in the modern sector and specifically, small and medium-size enterprises (SMEs) in manufacturing, transportation, construction, and a range of services that are non-traded. Their three sectors are thus: 'agriculture' (the Lewisian 'traditional' sector), 'open non-agriculture' (the Lewisian 'modern' sector), and a 'closed non-agriculture' sector (or Lewis' 'in-between' sector). The open non-agriculture sector is formal and includes tradeable non-agriculture activities including large-scale modern manufacturing as well as modern services. It is highly integrated into global markets (i.e. GVCs). This sector has new technological advantages and productivity levels close to or at international standards. In contrast, the closed non-agriculture or in-between sector is different and has informal and non-tradeable characteristics while lacking new technologies. It includes micro, small, and medium-size enterprises of the informal and non-tradeable economy. In short, the closed non-agriculture sector produces for domestic markets. Lewis (1979) argued that such 'in-between' enterprises play important developmental roles meeting domestic market needs and providing jobs. In this case, when the modern/GVC sector fails to expand sufficiently to absorb workers. In fact, if deindustrialization occurs in the large-scale, formal, tradeable, GVC-participating manufacturing sector, then the in-between sector may provide intermediate labour absorption especially so if informal urban services are already 'bloated' with labour and thus low wages. At this point, Furtado's (1969) understanding of non-unified or segmented labour markets is highly relevant. In contemporary times, there is a split of the labour market into one for low-skilled, informal manufacturing and one for medium- and high-skilled, formal manufacturing connected to GVCs.

Fourth, the final component of the theory of global inequality and its persistence relates to the intense competition between numerous developing countries which contend with each other to be suppliers in the relatively lower-value-added mid-range of the chain. In contrast to pre-1990, national economic development for developing countries is one of a relatively small number of globally competitive national manufacturing supplier firms supplying components to GVCs rather than the development of industries and the manufacture of entire goods. Developing countries are in direct competition with each other—that is, perhaps 40 to 50 or so middle-income countries that have domestic suppliers who are competitive internationally. Their competition is based on quality, reliability, and—given manufacturing is typically labour-intensive—labour costs in production. Some developing countries may be excluded from markets due to other developing countries' success or dominance in specific markets. Indeed, over time, manufacturing activity has been spread thinner and thinner across a growing number of developing countries (see Felipe et al., 2014, 2018). This makes it harder for each individual country to capture sufficient activity to achieve and sustain economic development. As observed by Haraguchi et al. (2017), this phenomenon is especially prominent in early or 'first stage' industrialization sectors such as textiles and apparel, as there is intense competition amongst late developing countries to gain employment shares in the global garment manufacturing industry. Relatedly, 'China's awakening' has had consequences for other developing countries. Since its entry into the WTO in the early 2000s, China has sucked up much of the labour-intensive work within GVCs, meaning fewer opportunities for other developing countries to slot into GVCs. In short, there is a Gerschenkronian argument that each successful industrializer fundamentally changes the global economy for those subsequently seeking industrialization. Further, some authors argue that exposure to Chinese imports is one of the additional drivers of deindustrialization in the developing world because of the difficulty for domestic companies of competing with Chinese imports (Cáceres, 2017; Jenkins, 2015a, 2015b; López, 2017; Nazeer and Rasiah, 2016).

In this context, developing countries can seek to enact or develop industrial policy in the same way China and other East Asian countries have done in so far that it is compatible with membership in the World Trade Organization (WTO), which is required to attract the lead TNCs who orchestrate GVCs. Wade (2014, pp. 793–4; see also Wade, 2018) points to the fact that a 'developmental state Mark I' can no longer create an autonomous industrial base due to TNCs' contemporary control of much of the global value chains and WTO rules on traditional industrial policy. However, a 'developmental state Mark II' is still possible because global rules such as those of the WTO do not constrain certain types of policies such as competitive devaluations, investment incentives, trade finance, and export taxes. Thus, the state can still act strategically. The renaissance of state-owned enterprises (SOEs) in countries facing stalled industrialization and premature deindustrialization, and the emergence of a 'new developmentalism' are signs of attempts at re-industrialization in the face of stalled industrialization and premature deindustrialization (see Kim and Sumner, 2020 for further discussion and also Chapter 6 in this book).

In sum, a theory of global inequality and its reproduction can be constructed from four components. First, the dynamics of a GVC world. Second, where developing countries are situated in that GVC world. Third, the dualism of contemporary economic development. Fourth, the 'energy' driving the system, namely intense competition between numerous middle-income developing countries which makes it harder for each country to capture enough to achieve sustained economic development.

4.5 Conclusion

This chapter has discussed the third great transformation, specifically the fragmentation of global production into GVCs. The literature on the impact of a GVC world on developing countries has been discussed. Moreover, the empirics of GVC participation have been considered. The myth that if developing countries integrate more and more in GVCs, the process will drive and sustain economic development in the longer term has been critiqued. Furthermore, theory has been developed to understand the relationship between a GVC world, deindustrialization, and global inequality.

The chapter has presented a set of arguments: first, that the primary drivers of stalled industrialization and premature deindustrialization are the dynamics of a GVC world, where global production is increasingly fragmented and spread thinner and thinner across more and more countries. This fragmentation makes it harder for late developing countries to capture enough economic activity to achieve and later sustain substantial economic development and job creation. Furthermore, an increase in economic activity resulting from GVC integration could even negatively impact incomes since the intense competition between developing countries will ultimately exert downward pressure on the prices of manufacturing exports, thereby depressing real wage growth. Additional difficulties arise since late developing countries have little control over the governance of a GVC world, as lead firms tend to be based in OECD countries.

In Chapter 5, we turn to the fourth great transformation. Specifically, the rise of an immiserizing form of economic growth. We interrogate the assumption that if developing countries integrate more and more into GVC world, the process will lead to broad-based, equitable economic progress. We consider the relationship between deindustrialization, a GVC world and the other aspect of global inequality, the within-country component or national inequality. We discuss national income inequality and the labour share of the functional distribution of income. We revisit the seminal works of Kuznets in order to understand inequality dynamics during (de)industrialization and then develop theory to explain the connection between deindustrialization and upward pressure on national income inequality.

5
Income Inequality within Countries

Growth with Falling Labour Shares

5.1 Introduction

In Chapter 4, we focused on the between-country component of global inequality. We discussed the third great transformation since circa 1990 and how the changes in global production and the emergence of a GVC world have impacted developing countries. We examined the empirical evidence and discussed theory to understand the processes of stalled industrialization and the spectre of deindustrialization in developing countries.

To recap, we argued the following: first, that stalled industrialization and premature deindustrialization are driven by the dynamics of a GVC world where global production is increasingly fragmented and spread across more and more countries. This makes it harder for individual developing countries to capture *sufficient* economic activity to sustain substantial economic progress, even a shallow economic development. Second, we showed that—on average—the benefits of joining GVCs are evident for low-income countries and diminish as countries reach middle-income. Third, we argued that four components are needed to explain the persistence of global inequality: the new global system itself; the position of developing countries within that system; the persistent dualism of developing countries' economies; and the intense competition between numerous middle-income developing to capture enough value-added and employment to sustain economic progress.

In this chapter, we consider the fourth great transformation. This is the rise of an immiserizing form of economic growth. We focus on what stalled industrialization and premature deindustrialization mean for the other new middle, the new, precarious middle of people and specifically what stalled industrialization and premature deindustrialization mean for intra-country inequality. We define immiserizing growth as economic growth with squeezed

Deindustrialization, Distribution, and Development: Structural Change in the Global South. Andy Sumner, Oxford University Press.
© Andrew Sumner 2021. DOI: 10.1093/oso/9780198853008.003.0005

labour shares, weak employment growth, and expansion of the informal sector.[1]

Moreover, there is the fourth myth of economic development. Specifically, that if developing countries integrate more and more into GVC world, the process will lead to broad-based, equitable economic development. We argue instead that GVC participation is driving immiserizing growth. Furthermore, GVC participation is squeezing labour shares as attempts are made to maintain international competitiveness in labour costs and fewer jobs are created relative to productivity gains than was historically the case. These processes then push more and more labour towards the less equal, informal manufacturing, and informal service sectors, exacerbating gross income inequality yet further.

In this chapter, we approach income inequality as a function of dualism like Lewis, Kuznets, and Furtado did and discuss both within- and between-sector inequality. If labour moves from a higher wage and more equal sector—such as formal manufacturing—to a less equal sector—such as informal manufacturing or informal services, gross income inequality is likely to rise overall. Meanwhile, what happens to net inequality is a political choice. Developing countries may seek to maintain international competitiveness by squeezing labour costs in wages or employment growth. This in itself will push labour more towards the less equal, informal manufacturing, and informal service sectors. In short, we argue that the GVC-driven process of stalled industrialization and premature deindustrialization of employment in MICs will increase gross income inequality by putting downward pressure on the labour share of income. The myth of broad-based economic progress is thus flawed.

This chapter is structured as follows: Section 5.2 revisits thinking on structural transformation and income inequality. Section 5.3 assesses the empirical evidence on the association between the stalled industrialization and deindustrialization that GVC world has engendered and national income inequality in developing countries. Section 5.4 then develops theory to explain the relationship between a GVC world, stalled industrialization and premature deindustrialization, and declining labour shares within countries. Section 5.5 concludes.

---

[1] This is not the first time immiserizing growth has been linked to GVCs. Kaplinksy (2014, p. 112) refers to an immiserizing growth whereby developing countries could find that an increase in economic activity—more output or more employment—could be associated with stagnant or falling real wages due to easy entry competition from developing countries in markets for ever lower-value-added goods. Additionally, increasing economic activity could be accompanied by falling prices of some developing countries' manufacture exports, resonating with Lewis' (2015) prophecy that a dependency on primary commodities would simply be replaced with a dependency on a small number of manufactures.

5.2   Structural Transformation and Income Inequality within Countries

Any discussion of national income inequality and economic development inevitably includes the seminal work of Kuznets (1955) and of Lewis (1954) on the inequality dynamics of the dual economy model as well as Furtado's (1964 [1961], 1965, 2020 [1974]) thinking. Specifically, the labour transition between 'sectors', which could be Lewis' traditional and modern sectors or Kuznets' rural and urban sectors or Furtado's backwards and nucleus sectors. The commonality is: There is one sector which is lower productivity and low-tech with surplus labour and another sector with higher productivity, high-tech, and a deficit of labour. Labour moves from the former to the latter sector, leading to economic development for Lewis and Kuznets or stagnation for Furtado. Rising gross income inequality is another commonality across Lewis, Kuznets, and Furtado.

Furtado's (1964 [1961], 1965, 2020 [1974]) view was that the importation of labour-saving technology from advanced countries and developing countries' dependence on that technology would mean more capital-intensive production in the nucleus sector and thus an increasing surplus of labour. As a result, national inequality would increase. The process of income concentration accompanied by external dependence on technology would strangle future growth, leading to stagnation and rising inequality. Furthermore, the focus on industrialization led by modernization and the importation of elite consumption patterns or the 'American way of life'—as Furtado put it (1983b [1978])—rather than industrialization based on the consumption of the masses would mean further income concentration.

Lewis (1954, 1976, 1979) too argued—implicitly in some places and explicitly in others—that gross income inequality would rise during economic development. Lewis argued that economic development required non-declining capital share of income for reinvestment purposes and this implies a steady or declining labour share of income. Thus, individual income inequality would rise (given its inverse association with the labour share), at least up to the Lewis turning point of the exhaustion of surplus labour in the traditional sector. Inequality would also rise initially because economic development does not start simultaneously across a country but is spatially focused, Lewis argued. He noted that:

> growth takes place in enclaves, surrounded by traditional activities...Development must be inegalitarian because it does not start in every part of an economy at the same time. Somebody develops a mine and employs a thousand people. Or

farmers in one province start planting cocoa, which will grow only in 10 per cent of the country. Or the Green Revolution arrives, to benefit those farmers who have plenty of rain or access to irrigation, while offering nothing to the other 50 per cent in drier regions.   (Lewis, 1976, p. 26)

It was the case for Lewis that a larger share of profits in national income would mean more resources for capital formation but as Lewis (1954, pp. 157–8) noted:

[t]he central fact of economic development is that the distribution of incomes is altered in favour of the saving class...All that the workers get out of the expansion is that more of them are employed at a wage above the subsistence earnings.

When the Lewis turning point is reached and surplus labour is exhausted, wages would rise and the functional distribution of income would move in favour of labour. At that point, labour markets would be unified rather than dualistic. The role of the state was considered to be important because if gross inequality rises during the Lewis transition, then public policy intervention is needed. Lewis (1979, pp. 212, 216) argued:

the Gini coefficient may actually show a rise in inequality, since the share of national output accruing to the bottom 50 per cent may fall... To tax its developed sectors and subsidize its underdeveloped sectors is one of the most powerful ways that a government can use to ensure the benefits of development... The moral for policy makers is of course not to rely on trickle down to benefit the traditional sector, but to attack the problems of that sector directly.

Lewis argued the turning point—where surplus labour was exhausted and wages would rise—could be delayed by matters related to the global economy. These matters were not discussed in Kuznets' (1955) paper, to which we will turn shortly and which did not cover open economy dynamics. Lewis noted international migration or *capital export* (i.e. a GVC world) would increase the labour surplus available (in the case of the opening of the economies of China and India by billions of people).

Lewis (1976), like Kuznets, discussed the relationship between economic development and distribution as one based on within- and between-sector inequality. He argued that the growth of the modern sector, or the 'enclave sector' as he calls it in the 1976 paper, has good and bad impacts on the traditional sector (p. 27). Notably, the enclave/modern sector may enrich the traditional sector by buying commodities and services from it, providing employment to those in the traditional sector, sending remittances, selling goods and services cheaper, and by developing infrastructure and public goods. Furthermore, through an example of new ideas and institutions, the enclave/modern sector can modernize the traditional sector. Whether development leads to widening inequality depends, in part, he argued, on how the traditional sector is able to respond to the new economic opportunities. For Lewis inegalitarian development, as the quote above shows, is not only the failure of 'trickle down' vertically from rich to poor but the failure to 'trickle along' or horizontally spread the benefits from enclave to traditional sectors. In fact, as Lewis (1976) noted, the traditional sector may see income stagnate because the enclave may be predatory (e.g. driving people off their land), products may compete with traditional trades, because of geographical polarization (the enclave attracts 'best brains' and capital), because population growth accelerates due to improved public health reducing the death rate, and/or because of excessive migration from the countryside. Lewis (1976, p. 29) concludes that whether the enclave/modern sector enriches the traditional sector or not 'probably depends most on whether the government coerces or helps the traditional sector, and on the nature of the enclaves'.

In contrast, Kuznets' (1955) thinking on structural transformation and income inequality is based on a two-sector economy model but the labour transition is from 'rural' to 'urban' sectors during the process of industrialization. Inequality rises in the early stages of development because the early benefits of growth would go to those with capital and education. As more people move out of the rural sector, real wages rise in the urban sector and inequality would fall. Kuznets argued that income inequality in a dual-sector economy is thus an aggregation of (i) inequality in each sector, (ii) the mean income of each sector, and (iii) the population shares in each sector. Thus, even the population shift itself could lead to rising gross inequality as Kuznets himself noted. Furthermore, although inequality may rise as a result of movement between sectors, this change in between-sector inequality may be balanced or outweighed by what happens to the within-sector components and the shares of each sector. Thus, initial inequality between and within sectors will play a role in outcomes.

For Kuznets the thesis of an 'upswing' in inequality is based on time-series data for the US, the UK, and two German states, and point estimates for India, Puerto Rico, and Ceylon. Kuznets (1955, pp. 6–7) held a belief that two forces would increase gross inequality: specifically, the concentration of savings in the upper-income group and the transfer of labour from the rural/

agricultural sector, which is more equal, to the urban/manufacturing one, which is a less equal sector. He suggested that the poorest lost out more rapidly than other groups, as income-expanding opportunities arose away from agriculture. Less well recognized is that Kuznets' 'downswing' was not based on data but on an abstract arithmetic model (Kanbur, 2017). Kuznets was clear that politics have the potential to counter-balance any increase in inequality. As Kuznets put it:

> One group of factors counteracting... is legislative interference and 'political' decisions. These may be aimed at limiting the capital accumulation of property directly through inheritance taxes and other explicit capital levies. They may produce similar effects indirectly....All these interventions, even when not directly aimed at limiting the effects of capital accumulation of past savings in the hands of the few, do reflect the view of society on the long-term utility of wide income inequalities.... Furthermore, in democratic societies the growing political power of the urban lower-income groups led to a variety of protective and supporting legislation.   (Kuznets, 1955, pp. 8–9, 16–17)

Kuznets argued that the only way to offset the rise in inequality was an increase in the share of income accruing to lower-income groups in non-agriculture. He further contended that, in democracies, urban migrants would become politically organized, leading to redistribution. Although Kuznets said little on the open-economy dynamics, there has been a set of contemporary scholars building new theory in the Kuznetsian tradition, many of whom have focused on such issues.

Contemporary scholars have developed theory with a focus on the impact of the global economy via commodity prices, interest rates, and agrarian liberalization; as well as aspects of national political economy and the distribution of land. Galbraith (2011), for example, argues that it is global forces—commodity prices and interest rates—that have driven the changes in national inequality since 1970. He reasons that a commodity boom reduces national inequality in countries with a dominant agricultural sector because it raises the relative income of farmers, while higher interest rates are bad for debtor countries and thus increase national inequality.

In a somewhat similar vein, at least in the sense of a focus on open economies, Lindert and Williamson (2001) argue that it is the shift of market orientation (from domestic to export) of agriculture that causes inequality to rise. Lindert and Williamson predict an initial rise in inequality after liberalization because income in the urban sector outpaces rises in income in the rural sector as agriculture shifts to market orientation.

Oyvat (2016) also argues that it is agrarian drivers—national land-ownership patterns—that are deterministic. Consistent with Lewis and Kuznets, he argues that migration is driven by higher urban incomes and this suppresses wages in the urban sector. If land inequality is higher, more people will migrate for lower wages as they do not own land or own small plots, and rural incomes are lower which will further depress urban wages.[2]

Finally, Acemoglu and Robinson (2002) argue—consistent with Kuznets—that when the process of industrialization does increase inequality, this leads to political mobilization of the masses that are concentrated in urban areas and factories. Political elites thus undertake reform to ensure their continued position at the top of society. The extension of the franchise is the best option for elites as it acts as a commitment to future redistribution and thus prevents unrest.

In sum, revisiting the thinking of Furtado, Lewis, and Kuznets on dualism and inequality provides useful heuristics for thinking about income inequality dynamics during structural transformation. Those writing since have broadened thinking with a focus on the open economy aspects of inequality and dual sector models. However useful as all of these theories are, they all assume a specific labour transition as the norm, namely the transition of labour from agriculture/rural/low productivity sectors to manufacturing/urban/higher productivity sectors. However, what if labour moves from manufacturing/urban/higher productivity sectors towards lower productivity informal manufacturing or to low productivity, informal services? What then are the inequality dynamics of the new varieties of structural transformation? We turn to this next.

5.3 The Empirics of Structural Change and Within-Country Inequality

What is the empirical evidence on the association between the stalled industrialization and deindustrialization that GVC world has engendered and national income inequality in developing countries? There are very few studies

---

[2] Empirically, Oyvat argues that the level of land inequality has a significant impact on urbanization, intra-urban inequality, and overall inequality. The results suggest that rural change—i.e. land reforms or subsidies to rural smallholders—would reduce urban inequality. Oyvat argues that agrarian structures in Asia tend to have more owner-cultivators and tenants and thus small- and medium-scale family farms than Latin America or sub-Saharan Africa, which tend to have high land inequality and large plantation structures that hire wage labour, and very small family farms. Thus, in Latin America and sub-Saharan Africa, the lack of sufficient formal employment opportunities for migrants generates an urban reserve army of labour in the urban subsistence sector, which depresses wages in the urban modern/capitalist sector.

that are relevant to assessing the within-country empirics of income inequality and stalled industrialization, deindustrialization, and tertiarization (virtually all tests of the Kuznets hypothesis assess the growth-inequality relationship instead). In one relevant empirical work, Angeles (2010) takes 4,000 observations of the Gini coefficient from the UNU-WIDER WIID database, covering most countries over five decades, and tests the effect of a change in non-agricultural employment shares on income/consumption inequality with panel data analysis (the percentage of labour employed in non-agriculture and the share of urban population). Angeles finds mixed results: Support for Kuznets is dependent on country groupings while country-by-country analysis does not support the Kuznets hypothesis.

More recently, Baymul and Sen (2020) focus on movement of labour between economic sectors and the consequences of this movement for income inequality using a standardized UNU-WIDER WIID and the GGDC 10-Sector Database of Timmer et al. (2015) (as we use in this book). In doing so, they re-examine the Kuznets hypothesis using economic sectors somewhat closer to what Kuznets (1955, p. 1) called his 'statistical pipe dream' of data he would have liked to have at his fingertips. Baymul and Sen remind us that Kuznets argued that inequality is composed of between- and within-sector components, and that inequality rises in the early stages of economic development as labour moves from a low average income sector with lower within-sector inequality—i.e., agriculture—to a higher average income sector with higher within-sector inequality—i.e., manufacturing. Baymul and Sen (2020, p. 1645) put it thus:

> The Kuznets process of widening inequality with structural transformation (that is, movement of workers away from agriculture) can be described as composed of two sub-processes: i) between-sector inequality: a movement of the population from a sector characterised by lower mean income to a sector characterised by higher mean income, and ii) within-sector inequality: the movement of the population from a sector with low within-sector inequality to a sector with higher within-sector inequality. If both sub-processes work in the same direction – that is, if the movement of workers is from a sector with both a low mean and low variance in incomes to a sector with a higher mean and high variance in incomes, then structural transformation will unambiguously increase inequality. However, if the movement of workers is from a sector with low mean income but higher variance of income to a sector with a higher mean income but lower variance in income, then it is less obvious that inequality will necessarily increase.

Heterogeneity plays a novel role in Baymul and Sen's approach in that they differentiate between three types of countries—structurally underdeveloped (where most people are employed in agriculture, typically LICs), structurally developing (where the proportion of workers in services is higher than that in agriculture, though the share of workers in agriculture is still higher than that in manufacturing, typically MICs), and structurally developed (where the proportion of workers in manufacturing is higher than that in agriculture, typically HICs).

Baymul and Sen concur that for many developing countries, the common contemporary labour transition is one of tertiarization rather than from agriculture to manufacturing. They find too that, where it has happened, a labour transition towards manufacturing has been in general income-*equalizing*, irrespective of the type of country. In short, manufacturing-led structural transformation has unambiguously reduced income inequality, contrary to Kuznets' expectations. Lewis too may have been surprised, given that the Lewis model is predicated on a non-declining capital share (implying rising income inequality by empirical association). Conversely, Baymul and Sen find the labour transition to services is unequalizing in structurally developing countries (i.e. MICs) and equalizing for structurally developed countries (i.e. HICs).

Baymul and Sen (2020, p. 1658) also consider the inequality consequences of labour movements to modern and to traditional services (which they label as 'business services' and 'non-business services'). They find that business services increase inequality in the structurally developing countries (i.e. MICs), though decrease inequality in structurally developed countries (i.e. HICs) while there is no clear impact on structurally underdeveloped countries (i.e. LICs). In terms of the Kuznetsian model of between- and within-county inequality, Baymul and Sen (p. 1464) theorize that labour-intensive manufacturing exhibits low within-sector inequality, is factory- and formal sector-based, thus minimum wages and labour regulations are more likely leading to wage compression. In contrast, the service sector is usually dominated by self-employment, poor pay, and informality (e.g. trade, hotels and restaurants) alongside high-paid jobs in formal services (such as banking and finance). In sum, a movement of labour to services will exacerbate within-sector inequality in services more so than a movement of labour to manufacturing.

In keeping with these discussions, we follow Baymul and Sen using our own groupings that we used in previous chapters and split 'services' between a Lewisian modern sector of higher productivity services and a Lewisian traditional sector of lower-productivity services. We discuss the findings next.

We analyse the consequences of industrialization and deindustrialization for within-country income inequality in developing countries. It is argued that, consistent with Baymul and Sen, not only are rising manufacturing shares equalizing but they are dramatically so in the developing as well as the developing and former developing countries groups. Furthermore, rising shares in Lewisian modern services are unequalizing in developing countries; and expanding shares of Lewisian traditional services are initially unequalizing though later equalizing.

We next utilise, with grateful thanks Baymul and Sen's dataset. As before, the country groupings are: (i) the full sample (all countries), (ii) developed countries (countries which became HICs before 1990), (iii) developing countries (current LICs and MICs), and (iv) developing and former developing countries (LICs, MICs, and countries which have become HICs post-1990).

We take the employment share (as a share of the total employment) and output share (which is measured as the value-added share of the GDP) in constant prices for six economic sectors. Subsequently, we consider the income inequality consequences of changes in the shares of each of those economic sectors. The six economic sectors are as follows: agriculture, mining, manufacturing, utilities/construction, and—as noted above—the two service sectors. We differentiate between the higher-value-adding or 'Lewisian' modern services of financial intermediation, renting, and business activities, which we label FIRE services and the lower-value-adding or 'Lewisian' traditional services of trade, transport, government, and personal services, which we label non-FIRE services.

To explore the relationship between these sectoral shares and income inequality, we follow the approach of Baymul and Sen (2020).[3] The only difference is that we use six economic sectors while they consider manufacturing, non-manufacturing (utilities, construction, and mining), and services (and make reference to two service sectors in the discussion). In all figures below, the horizontal axis depicts sectoral shares (of employment or value-added) and the vertical axis shows gross income inequality measured in the gross Gini coefficient. Figure 5.1 covers employment shares. Figure 5.2 examines value-added shares.

---

[3] Baymul and Sen (2020) add data for low-income African countries from Mensah et al. (2018). The difference between the replication in this book is that we add value added shares (in constant prices) from the GGDC 10-Sector database and we remove the Mensah et al., (2018) countries for comparability with the dataset used in Chapter 3. The sample is as follows: Full sample = 40 countries (352 observations); Developed countries 14 countries (138 observations); developing and former countries = 30 countries (249 observations); developing countries = 26 countries (214 observations).

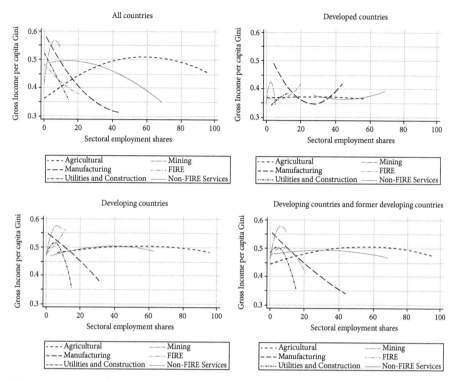

Figure 5.1 Sectoral employment shares and gross income inequality.

Note: Mensah et al.'s (2018) countries were removed to ensure comparability with the dataset used in Chapter 3. The figures follow for comparability those of Baymul and Sen (2020) and thus are fitted values based on a quadratic relationship between the Gini and the employment shares or value-added.

Source: Author based on Baymul and Sen (2020) dataset which is drawn from GGDC 10-Sector database and a standardized version of UNU-WIDER (forthcoming) WIID.

What does the data say? We can once again make a set of empirical observations or stylized facts.[4] The plots for gross and net income inequality are very similar because tax and transfers, in general, make surprisingly little difference to gross and net income inequality in many developing countries (see Lustig et al., 2017); thus, we present the plots here for the gross Gini (i.e. before policy interventions).

First, employment shares: Figure 5.1 shows that a rise in the sectoral shares of manufacturing is equalizing in the full sample, in the developing countries sub-sample and in the developing and former group. In both the developing country and developing/former countries and sub-samples, we can see that while the expansion of manufacturing is equalizing, Non-FIRE services are initially unequalizing to a small degree and then equalizing later. FIRE

---

[4] For further discussion see Sumner (2021).

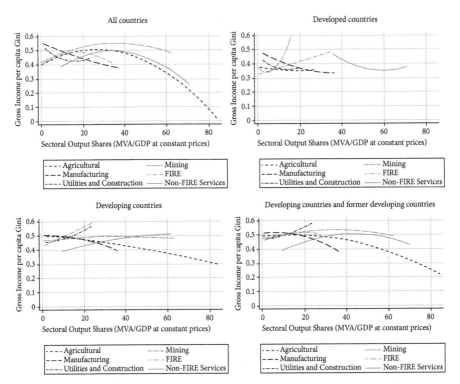

Figure 5.2 Sectoral output shares (constant prices) and gross income inequality.

Notes: Mensah et al.'s (2018) countries were removed to ensure comparability with the dataset used in Chapter 3. The figures follow for comparability those of Baymul and Sen (2020) and thus are fitted values based on a quadratic relationship between the Gini and the employment shares or value-added.

Source: Author based on Baymul and Sen (2020) dataset with value-added shares added from GGDC 10-Sector database.

services are very unequalizing in developing countries though in developing/former follow an inverted-U shape.

Second, value-added shares: In Figure 5.2, the value-added shares of sectors show that manufacturing again is equalizing in the whole sample, in the developing country group as well as in the developing/former countries group. In the whole sample, inverted-U curves are evident for FIRE, and non-FIRE services shares. In the developing countries group, although rising manufacturing shares are equalizing, expanding FIRE services and non-FIRE services shares are unequalizing. In the developing/former group inverted-U shapes are evident for FIRE services and non-FIRE services.

In sum, we find that expanding manufacturing shares are equalizing in developing countries and that the process of tertiarization is predominantly unequalizing in current developing countries, especially so the expansion of modern (FIRE) services. Expanding shares of traditional (non-FIRE) services may initially be unequalizing though later more equalizing. We can thus conclude that the kind of structural change that GVC world has engendered is likely to be associated with upward pressure on gross inequality at least for a time. In the following section we develop theory to explain the relationship between a GVC world, stalled industrialization and premature deindustrialization, and pressure on gross inequality within developing countries. The question that arises from this point is why does it matter if contemporary structural change is unequalizing within developing countries? In the next section it is argued that it matters intrinsically and also because it challenges the idea that if developing countries integrate more and more into GVC world, the process of integration will drive broad-based and equitable economic development. In the following section we thus develop theory to explain the relationship between a GVC world, stalled industrialization and premature deindustrialization, and rising inequality within developing countries.

5.4 Beyond the Fourth Myth of Economic Development

The myth accompanying the fourth transformation is that if developing countries integrate more and more into GVC world, the process of integration will drive broad-based and equitable economic development. In fact, the structural transformation that GVC integration has engendered is associated upward pressure on gross income inequality. This section develops theory to explain the relationship between stalled industrialization and premature deindustrialization, GVC world, and the within-country component of global inequality. In the previous chapter we outlined a set of four components to a theory to explain the between-country aspect of global inequality. Specifically, the new global system and its dynamics, the position of developing countries in that system, the dualism of developing countries' economies, and the intense competition between developing countries to capture value-added and employment from the mid-range of the same kinds of GVCs. The same set of components also explains the within-country aspect of global inequality. We discuss each.

First, the new global system itself is predicated on squeezing labour shares and thus upward pressure on national income inequality. Second, this is because of the position of developing countries in that system as dependent on modern, labour-saving technology provided via GVCs. Third, the dualism of developing economies leads to squeezed labour shares during a bifurcated tertiarization towards modern services with little employment growth and towards traditional services with low wages. Finally, the competition between MICs to capture value-added and employment in the same set of GVC entry points and GVCs entails a shift in the balance of power between capital and labour in favour of capital.

First, we discuss the new global system and its predication on falling labour shares. It is important to note that rising individual income inequality is strongly associated with a falling labour share in cross-country analysis (see Bengtsson and Waldenström, 2018; Dao et al., 2017a, 2017b; Daudey and Garcia-Penalosa, 2007). Erauskin (2020), for example, considers the 1990–2015 period with data for 62 developed and developing countries and finds a lower labour share is strongly associated with a higher Gini coefficient and shows this is because a lower labour share is strongly associated with smaller income shares for the poorest 40 per cent and a larger income share for the highest quintile. Lower labour shares are strongly associated with higher income inequality across and over time within countries because capital ownership is usually concentrated in the top of the distribution and thus higher returns to capital tend to raise inequality.

Furthermore, estimates of labour shares consistently show falling labour shares since *circa* 1990 in particular. In short, the assumption that capital and labour shares are constant during growth (which is based on Kaldor, 1961 and Keynes, 1939 who argued that this was a long-run phenomenon) no longer holds empirically. The downward trend in labour shares is well documented (see, for example, Elsby, Hobijn, and Sahin, 2013; Karabarbounis and Neiman, 2014; Piketty, 2014; Piketty and Zucman, 2014). One systematic investigation of Guerriero (2019), based on data for 1970–2015 and according to six different measures, finds that there is an unambiguous declining trend from about 1990 onwards. She rejects the argument that changes in labour shares are due to poor or no adjustment for self-employed income, indirect tax, and capital depreciation.[5] Stockhammer (2017) concurs that labour shares have declined substantially in both OECD countries and most developing countries over the period 1970–2007.

The link between GVC integration and falling labour shares is as follows: GVC participation raises the overall capital intensity of production and weakens the collective power of labour via the implicit threat of switching suppliers. The World Bank (2020) concurs that GVC participation is

---

[5] The labour share is usually estimated as the total compensation to employees divided by national income. National income needs to be adjusted for taxes on production and imports (minus subsidies) and capital income must be adjusted for capital depreciation. It is important to note here that labour income shares are subject to considerable contention on measurement (see for discussion, Guerriero (2019) who presents six different measures), especially so due to 'mixed' income of the self-employed and also indirect taxes and capital depreciation.

associated with rising inequality and falling labour shares, noting that in 63 developed and developing countries, GVC integration contributed to a falling labour share between 1995 and 2011 and overall, GVCs were the largest single contributor to the fall of labour shares by percentage points.

Second, the position of developing countries in the global system is that of an importer of modern technology via GVCs. This technology is labour saving with reference to low-skilled labour. Timmer et al. (2014) find that the labour shares fell between 1995 and 2008 and consequentially, capital shares rose in developing countries by three percentage points from 55.2 per cent to 58.4 per cent. They also find that low-skilled labour shares (which represent the vast majority of the population) fell from 23.8 per cent to 17.5 per cent. In contrast, medium- and high-skilled labour shares (which represent a minority of the population of developing countries) rose respectively, from 15.6 per cent to 17.0 per cent, and from 5.4 per cent to 7.1 per cent between 1995 and 2008 (see Table 5.1).

In some developing countries, the changes were higher than in others. For example, capital shares rose by nine percentage points in China and five percentage points in India and Indonesia. In Brazil, the picture is more complicated as capital shares actually fell and although the labour share rose overall, there was a squeeze of the low-skilled labour shares. Across developing countries, low-skilled labour shares fell by 6 per cent. In Brazil, China, India, and Indonesia specifically, they decreased by between 5 and 9 per cent. Timmer et al. thus argue that most GVCs have a bias towards high-skilled labour. Moreover, they argue that developing countries—surprisingly given the abundance of labour—have focused on capital-intensive activities (and the capital share is rising) rather than low-skilled labour. Their data show the value-added share of high-skilled workers increased across most developing

Table 5.1 Changes in capital and labour shares, selected developing countries, 1995–2008

	Change in capital share	Change in labour shares		
		Low-skilled	Medium-skilled	High-skilled
India	4.5	−5.9	−1.7	3.1
China	9.3	−9.3	−2.1	2.0
Indonesia	5.3	−8.1	1.3	1.6
Brazil	−6.7	−4.8	7.5	4.0
Developing countries (World minus HICs)	3.2	−6.3	1.4	1.7

Source: Timmer et al. (2014, Table 4, p. 111) based on World Input-Output Database, November 2013.

countries. These data are consistent with the estimates by Rodrik (2016) and Kunst (2019), whereby stalled industrialization and premature deindustrialization are associated with the reduction of low-skilled employment.

The argument that the reduction of the wage share is technologically driven is predicated on the substitution of labour by capital and, as the above data shows, in particular the substitution of low-skilled labour (Berman, Bound, and Griliches, 1994; Berman, Bound, and Machin, 1998; Cowen, 2013; Brynjolfsson and McAfee, 2014; Goldin and Katz, 2009). If capital and labour *are* substitutes, an increase in the capital intensity of production will lead to a falling labour share.

The technology explanation points towards labour-saving technology as a driver of deindustrialization of employment, resonating with Furtado. Theories of 'skill-biased technical change' (e.g. Berman et al., 1998; Card and DiNardo, 2002; Johnson, 1997; Piva et al., 2005) have argued that highly skilled workers benefit more from new technology, such as Information and Communication Technology, and that new technology displaces low-skilled jobs. In short, there is a shift in the occupational structure in terms of skills: the higher the skills, the higher its demand. Consequently, high-skill employment will rise while low-skill employment will decline. Put another way, technological changes have raised the productivity of high-skilled labour relatively more than low-skilled labour or the new technologies of ICT have increased returns from skills (Katz and Autor, 1999). Kunst (2019) finds that the employment lost due to premature deindustrialization is mostly unskilled labour and concurs that the employment losses occur in the formal manufacturing sector, and also notes that stalled industrialization and premature deindustrialization are driven by jobs vulnerable to ICT adoption.

A debate has ensued as to whether technical change is low-skilled labour substitution or routine labour substitution. To date this appears to be an OECD country issue, though there are some initial signs in some MICs.[6] It refers to the shift away from manual and routine cognitive work towards non-routine cognitive work (see especially Autor et al., 2003 and also Acemoglu and Autor, 2011; Goos and Manning, 2007; Goos, Manning, and Salomons, 2014; Goos, 2018; Harrigan, Reshef, and Toubal, 2016). Routine-bias unlike skill-biased technical change leads to job polarization—disappearing middle-skilled jobs—and is predicted to be a non-linear demand effect of

---

[6] Goos and Manning (2007) coined the term 'job polarization'. They showed that in the UK, over a thirty-year period, the occupations with the highest and lowest wages had increased whilst the middle-wage occupations had fallen. Others concurred: Autor et al. (2003) made similar findings for the US, Spitz-Oener (2006) for Germany, Adermon and Gustavsson (2015) for Sweden, and Green and Sand (2015) for Canada.

technological change (particularly new technologies) on the skills structure because computers, for example, tend to substitute routine tasks that generally belong to the category of medium-skilled jobs. Jobs that are manual or routine are likely to disappear, such as administrative or clerical jobs. In contrast, jobs that are manual and non-routine (typically low-skilled service sector) or cognitive and non-routine (typically high-skilled managerial/professional jobs) are less likely to disappear. Autor and Dorn (2013) argue that technological advancement is allowing for the automation of routine tasks in many highly productive industries and as a result, workers displaced are moving into the low-skilled service sector.

In developing countries so far, there is some evidence of routine-bias technical change though it is limited to date. Das and Hilgenstock (2018) analyse a cross-country panel and find that the polarization of incomes is related to this kind of technological advancement, but developing countries seem less vulnerable to it at least to date. However, Das and Hilgenstock do argue that structural transformation and greater involvement in GVCs are likely to lead to higher exposure to routinization (p. 23) and thus—in due course—rapidly rising routinization is likely to lead to labour market polarization. Das (2018) makes a similar argument with reference to a regional analysis for Asia. Specifically, there is an association between more exposure to routinization and a higher likelihood of ICT capital substituting mid-skilled labour employment which leads to a lower labour share of income. Existing exposure is low in developing Asia though this will likely grow in the years ahead. Das (p. 12) reiterates the positive association between more GVC participation and higher exposure to routinization. In other words, more participation in GVCs is associated with raised routine exposure in developing countries. In contrast, Maloney and Molina (2016) find no evidence of job polarization in developing countries using census data for 21 developing countries though do identify 'incipient polarization' in a few MICs, specifically Indonesia, Mexico, and Brazil. With a focus on GVCs directly and the use of a task-based model of production in GVCs, Reijnders and de Vries (2018) find that there is a growing share of non-routine jobs in total employment in the period 1999–2007 in advanced countries and some middle income developing countries including China, India, Brazil, Mexico, and Indonesia. They decompose the changes in the labour demand between offshoring and technological change. They find that technological change leads to a higher share of employment in non-routine jobs. Their findings point towards the fact that technological change within GVCs reduce demand for routine labour relative to non-routine labour. In sum, these are likely to be emerging issues for MICs in the years ahead.

Relatedly, it is evident that pre- and post-1990, meaning pre and post the emergence of GVC world, there are quite different patterns of productivity growth and employment growth. Heintz (2010) examined employment growth and the productivity growth rate in 35 countries between 1961 and 2008 and finds that increases in the productivity growth rate slow down the rate of employment growth, and that this pattern is getting stronger over time. In the 1960s, a one percentage point increase in the growth rate of productivity reduced employment growth by just 0.07 percentage points, indicating output and productivity increasing at almost the same rate. However, in the 2000s, that same one percentage point increase in the growth rate of productivity reduced employment growth substantially by 0.54 percentage points.

If we consider the most recent data from the GGDC 10-Sector Database (see Figure 5.3), we can assess the relationship between labour productivity growth and employment growth pre- and post-1990. The pre-1990 period shows a positive correlation between labour productivity growth and employment growth in both the full sample and in the developing country group. In short, more productivity growth is associated with more employment growth as Kaldor envisaged. However, the data in the post-1990 period show the opposite: more labour productivity growth is associated with declining employment growth in both the full sample and in the developing countries group. In other words, the post-1990 period is one where labour productivity growth is not associated with employment growth. This would support the argument of a move towards more capital-intensive production in the post-1990 period.

Third, the dualism of developing countries' economies is also relevant to labour shares because, as Suzuki et al. (2018) highlight, shifts between economic sectors impact the labour shares within those sectors and the overall labour shares. Some sectors, notably modern services such as FIRE services, tend to favour high-skilled labour. In contrast, agriculture, hotels, restaurants, and construction tend to be dominated by low-skilled labour. Utilities and manufacturing, wholesale and retail trade, mining, transportation, storage, and communication tend to be medium-skilled dominated sectors. Thus, the movement of labour to certain sectors—those that favour high-skilled workers—will in and of itself be unequalizing. Oishi and Paul (2018) further posit that the growth in low-skilled informal employment—i.e. in non-FIRE services—will entail a falling labour share overall.

Fourth, the intense price-based competition between developing countries to capture value-added and employment in a GVC world has also changed the national political economy in terms of the bargaining power of

Pre-1990

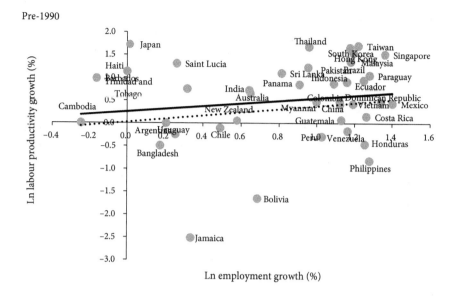

Post-1990

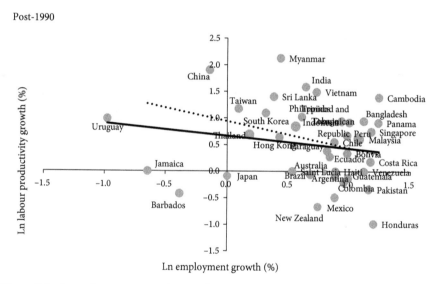

Figure 5.3 Annual average growth rate of employment and labour productivity (black line = all sample, dotted line = developing countries), pre-1990/post-1990.
Note: Productivity is calculated by dividing real GDP by number of persons engaged.
Source: Author based on GGDC 10-Sector database.

labour and capital in favour of the latter. In short, the labour share is driven by the power of the capitalist class to determine the capital share of income through investment and saving decisions (see e.g. Kaldor 1956, 1957). The capital share can be influenced by the saving propensity of workers, but it is fundamentally driven by the investment level of capitalists and/or capitalists' ability to pass any nominal increase in wages to the final consumers by raising prices. Furthermore, the capital share is strongly influenced by the price-setting power of capitalists, which in turn is determined by their market power (see e.g. Kalecki, 1954) and by labour market dynamics, industrial relations (i.e. union density), and workers' claim over total output. In a GVC world, the power of capitalists manifests in their ability to threaten to, or actually shift to, new suppliers in the same or a different country. Economic policies for Kalecki (1954) were influenced by the opposing interests of capitalists and workers. This distributional struggle has important implications since workers have a higher marginal propensity to consume. Thus, if there is spare capacity in the economy, an increase in workers' compensation can stimulate aggregate demand. However, if the reduction in profits reduces the savings and investments of capitalists below a certain threshold, long-term growth can be compromised. In terms of the empirics of labour shares, Stockhammer (2017), for example, finds the largest negative effects to be related to capital/labour relations and evident via globalization, austerity, and financialization (the increase in financial activity and prominence of financial institutions due to deregulation of financial markets and capital flows). He argues that factors affecting the bargaining position of labour, such as globalization—not only GVC participation but associated trade and capital account openness—mean greater capital mobility and weakened bargaining power of labour due to the threat to relocate. Hein and Mundt (2012) too argue that the liberalization process that started in the 1980s gave more market power to companies, allowing them to raise mark-ups and thus reduce the labour share (as a GVC world emerged).

In sum, we can build theory to explain the relationship between GVC world, structural change, and rising gross income inequality within countries. First, the new global system is predicated on reduced labour shares over time. Second, this is because modern technology provided via GVCs is labour-saving and especially so regarding low-skilled labour. Third, the dualism of developing economies means tertiarization leads to falling labour shares in and of itself. Finally, there is a shift in the relative power of capital vis-à-vis labour as result of the competition between MICs to capture value-added and employment.

5.5 Conclusion

This chapter has discussed the fourth great transformation since 1990—the rise of immiserizing growth—and thus the consequences of stalled industrialization and premature deindustrialization for global inequality. We revisited Furtado's, Lewis', and Kuznets' work on structural transformation and income inequality and noted that the sum of inequality relates to changes in both between- and within-sector components. We then considered the empirical evidence. Subsequently, we theorized about deindustrialization, income inequality, and a GVC world focusing on the functional distribution of income. We have argued that there is a causal link between a GVC world and stalled industrialization and premature deindustrialization in the developing world and relatedly, a rise in the within-country component of global inequality. The theory to explain this is based on four components: The new global system, developing countries' position within the new global system, economic dualism in developing countries, and a change in the balance of power between capital and labour.

We conclude with a set of Kaldorian stylized facts: First, deindustrialization and tertiarization towards the informal services sectors are associated with rises in income inequality. Second, on average, income inequality is negatively associated with the labour share so that when the labour share falls, income inequality increases. Third, the reduction of the labour share is a consequence of the emergence of a GVC world, developing countries' position in that world, the dualism of their economies, and the competition between developing countries to capture value-added and employment in modern manufacturing GVCs.

In the following, concluding Chapter 6, we outline the key arguments made across the book. Furthermore, we present the 'tertiary trilemma' that developing countries face and discuss the nascent 'new developmentalism' or state capitalism renaissance that is emerging as a result of stalled industrialization and premature deindustrialization.

6

Conclusion

6.1 Introduction

The intellectual contribution of the book has been to provide a detailed account of the contemporary processes of stalled industrialization, deindustrialization, and tertiarization as well as on their characteristics, drivers, and consequences in the developing world. Furthermore, the book has connected empirically and theoretically the phenomena of stalled industrialization, deindustrialization, and tertiarization, the emergence of a GVC world, and global inequality.

We began this book with Furtado's (2020 [1974]) myth of economic development. To recap, Furtado argued the myth was that the economic development of the advanced countries could be universalized and, as a consequence, poor peoples would one day have the lifestyles of those who are currently rich peoples. We noted Furtado wrote of this myth over forty years ago. This book has argued that there is a new mirage of economic development due to a set of system-wide transformations, each with an accompanying myth. The new mirage resonates with Furtado's thinking, though the characteristics of contemporary capitalism have changed and the global system has gone through a series of transformations since the end of the Cold War. The set of four inter-related, great transformations discussed have reshaped the global capitalist superstructure since the end of the Cold War. These transformations have reconfigured Furtado's myth into a complex, contemporary guise in terms of what is constraining the economic development of developing countries. The new mirage of economic development is due to the juxtaposition of this set of myths. Together, the illusion created is that most developing countries are on their way towards, and will some day resemble, the advanced countries in their structural characteristics, and poor peoples will catch up with the incomes of people in advanced countries.

A diminished form of economic development is instead the dominant pathway for developing countries today and that is a form of economic development that loses steam around middle-income. In this shallow economic development, a relatively small number of globally competitive domestic

Deindustrialization, Distribution, and Development: Structural Change in the Global South. Andy Sumner, Oxford University Press.
© Andrew Sumner 2021. DOI: 10.1093/oso/9780198853008.003.0006

companies in each country slot into global value chains. Hence, there are no longer attempts to build 'deep' economic development of extensive domestic industry.

The reshaping of the capitalist world economy superstructure, as outlined, is due to the set of co-evolving transformations. The first transformation relates to the economic growth and thus reduced significance of aid to most developing countries. Most developing countries have transitioned to middle-income countries. This means most developing countries, with the exception of a small group, have moved from aid-dependent to a situation where traditional aid is much less important. This substantial economic growth has generated an accompanying myth that economic development is ahistorical. This book has argued this is not the case. Instead it has been outlined that the concept of late development remains as crucial as ever in understanding contemporary development. As a consequence of the first transformation, many people are no longer living in absolute poverty, rather in a precarious position between poverty and security from future poverty.

A second transformation has been the emergence of stalled industrialization and premature deindustrialization. The myth accompanying this transformation is that economic development is sector-neutral. This book has argued this is not the case. Manufacturing-led economic development has special properties which make it preferable to tertiary-led economic development in the sense of delivering value-added as well as formal employment growth. These processes have led to a paradox of prematurity in the sense of premature deindustrialization and early tertiarization amid late economic development.

A third transformation is the change in the global economy whereby the global production process has been fragmented and dispersed across numerous countries. The myth accompanying this transformation is that for developing countries, more and more integration into GVC world will drive and sustain economic development in the long run to high income. This book has argued this is not the case. Developing countries have become peripheral suppliers to global value chains with the core or advanced countries largely remaining home to higher-value-added activities and the lead TNCs who orchestrate (though do not necessarily own) production.

Finally, there is a fourth transformation. This is the rise of an immiserizing form of growth, meaning growth with falling labour shares, and weakening employment growth in the modern/formal sector. The myth accompanying this transformation is that if developing countries integrate more and more into GVC world, the process will lead to broad-based, equitable economic development. This book has argued this is not the case. The Kuznetsian twist is that labour is moving from a higher wage and more equal sector of formal manufacturing to the less equal sectors of informal manufacturing or informal services.

The ultimate result of these transformations has been the dis-embedding of deep industrialization from the very idea of economic development. This book has shone light on these transformations and the resulting new mirage of economic development. The book has sought to understand and explain these new phenomena and their impact on the between-country and within-country components of global inequality. Manufacturing expansion in developing countries is key to reducing global inequality, both within and between countries, because the expansion of manufacturing value-added fuels faster economic growth and thus has the power to reduce between-country inequality. At the same time, manufacturing also has strong potential to expand employment opportunities and thus reduce the within-country component of global inequality. The book has argued that the fragmentation of global production into a GVC world is driving stalled industrialization and premature deindustrialization in middle-income developing countries and thus is threatening the future standards of living of the world's two new middles of countries and people. Looking ahead, the speedster economic development predicated on manufacturing that fuelled East Asia and the China model of economic development is unlikely to be repeatable. In fact, the signals point towards a future of tertiary-led growth which will be slower and unequalizing. Taken together, the slower catch-up of developing countries with developed countries and the upward pressure on within-country inequality due to stalled industrialization and deindustrialization suggest a global inequality boomerang in the next decade or so, where the declining trend of global inequality witnessed since the mid-2000s to the present will reverse.

In this concluding chapter, we summarize the book and its key arguments. Furthermore, we consider the economic development options available to developing countries ahead. In doing so, we outline the 'tertiary trilemma' that developing countries face and discuss the nascent 'new developmentalism' that is a response to the processes of stalled industrialization and premature deindustrialization.

This chapter is structured as follows: Section 6.2 summarizes the book. Section 6.3 outlines the book's set of stylized facts. Section 6.4 then looks ahead at developing countries' future options for economic development and responses to stalled industrialization and deindustrialization. Section 6.5 concludes.

6.2 A Recap

In this section, we summarize the contents of this book in order to situate the core arguments—or Kaldorian stylized facts—that follow. So, what has this book discussed? In the introductory chapter we outlined the focus and scope of the book. In Chapter 2, the first transformation. Specifically, the substantial economic growth and declining importance of aid in many developing countries and the consequential bifurcation of the developing world were discussed. An emerging polarization was noted and two new, precarious 'middles' identified. The chapter discussed the accompanying myth that economic development is sector-neutral and the relevance of the concept of late development to understanding the contemporary late economic development of developing countries.

In Chapter 3, we focused on the second transformation—the changing pattern of structural transformation—and why manufacturing still matters. The chapter discussed the accompanying myth that economic development is sector-neutral.

In Chapter 4, we turned to the third transformation—the fragmentation of global production—and the relationship between stalled industrialization, premature deindustrialization, and global inequality, with a focus on the between-country component of global inequality. We assessed research to date and made empirical estimates. Subsequently, we discussed the theoretical connection between a GVC world, stalled industrialization, and deindustrialization in the developing world. The chapter discussed the accompanying myth that more and more integration into GVC world will drive and sustain economic development in developing countries. Theory based on four components was presented to explain the reproduction of the between-country aspect of global inequality. Specifically, the structural evolution of the global system, how developing countries sit within the system, the persistent economic dualism of developing countries, and the intense competition between more and more middle-income developing countries over the same set of GVCs and GVC entry points to capture value-added and employment in order to achieve economic progress.

In Chapter 5, we focused on the fourth transformation—the evolution of growth into an immiserizing form—and the other aspect of global inequality, namely the within-country component. We discussed empirical evidence. The chapter discussed the accompanying myth that more and more integration into GVC world will drive and sustain equitable economic development in developing countries. The same set of four components that was presented to explain the reproduction of the between-country component of global inequality was then developed to also explain the reproduction of the within-country component of global inequality. Specifically, the new global system which is predicated on squeezing labour shares and thus rising pressure on gross national income inequality, the position of developing countries and their importing of labour-saving modern technology as part and parcel of GVC integration, the dualism of economies that squeezes labour shares via the process of bifurcated tertiarization, and the shift in the balance of power between capital and labour in favour of capital as a result of the competition between MICs to capture value-added and employment in the same set of GVC access points.

Finally, in this concluding chapter, we draw together the arguments of the book and lay out the strategic options for late economic development. We also look ahead to the fourth industrial revolution that is likely to accelerate the transformations we have outlined.

6.3   The Core Thesis and a Set of Stylized Facts

6.3.1   The Core Thesis

In this book the core thesis is this: Furtado's myth of late economic development remains evident albeit in a new guise. Specifically, the myth that developing countries will one day resemble advanced countries and poor people's lifestyles will resemble lifestyles of peoples in advanced countries. Developing countries can achieve some progress—as many have—but of a diminished nature. Typically, a relatively small number of domestic firms that are internationally competitive slot into global value chains, generating some value-added and—hopefully—employment growth at least up to productivity levels associated with middle income. Furthermore, pursuing even shallow industrialization, let alone deep industrialization, is getting harder and harder over time as more and more countries compete over the same access points of the same GVCs.

Underpinning the analysis, the concept of late development provides a means to understanding contemporary forms of new, shallow, and stunted economic development in developing countries. The concept of late development helps explain how late economic development has changed in characteristics over time. We echo Furtado's critique of Gerschenkron and argue that late developers have to face other countries that have already industrialized and are dominant in global industries and GVCs. Many of these global industries have achieved a high level of technological maturity and latecomers thus face competition on unfavourable terms with established countries.

Moreover, late developers experience fewer employment generation benefits than earlier industrializers. Modern technology can be accessed through GVC participation but on unfavourable terms of non-ownership or borrowing that must be paid for in the form of patent and fee costs. It is clear that benefits from GVC participation can be realized at lower levels of per capita income. However, those benefits are—on average—not sustained beyond productivity levels associated with middle-income countries, and job creation in the Lewisian modern sector becomes limited. For each developing country, it becomes increasingly difficult to extract sufficient production for the modern sector to sustain long-run economic development. Additionally, developing countries have little control over the governance of the contemporary GVC world as they are, at best, semi-peripheries within GVC world where lead TNCs are mostly headquartered in the core OECD countries. A caveat: this story is one of the average developing country. Of course, it is possible that an individual country or a small number of countries could dominate GVC entry points and so capture most of the value-added and employment and thus achieve economic progress, albeit at the expense of many other developing countries.

Competition between developing countries for a share in lower-productivity activities within GVCs will ultimately exert downward pressure on the prices of the manufacturing exports that these activities produce, thereby dragging down wages. This will lead to a new kind of immiserizing growth that entails falling labour shares, and weak formal sector employment creation. Moreover, developing countries are excluded from the more profitable tasks within GVCs since those tasks tend to be already dominated by developed countries due to world class universities in the creative industries and sciences as well as their long-established TNCs that lead GVCs.

In short, the benefits of joining GVCs are clearer for low-income countries, then shrink for middle-income countries. In contrast, GVC participation is beneficial for high-income countries, as leading companies from high-income countries take advantage of low-income or middle-income countries in GVCs through their oligopolistic market power. However, most of today's MICs will struggle to reach high-income levels, judging by their manufacturing peaks versus the manufacturing peaks of earlier industrializers, and the association between manufacturing peaks and attaining high-income levels. As a consequence of the above, a new kind of dependency or subordination of a semi-periphery is evident. As Lewis (1976) foresaw, the rapid advancements in specific sectors within the developing world have sparked a new export dependency on a small number of manufacture exports or tasks, which have replaced older dependencies on a small number of primary commodity exports.

6.3.2　Ten Stylized Facts

There is a set of stylized facts or supporting arguments to the core thesis. These stylized facts relate to each of the transformations and thus add to the outlined above. The first stylized fact is that there has been substantial economic growth in the developing world since the Cold War.

A second stylized fact is that a new polarization has emerged between very poor and aid-dependent developing countries or a periphery on the one hand and MICs or a semi-periphery on the other hand. The former, low or zero growth and aid-dependent countries have barely begun on the pathway to industrialization. The latter have industrialized to some considerable extent, although this is now under threat from stalled industrialization and the spectre of premature deindustrialization.

A third stylized fact is that the polarization noted has produced two new 'middles'. There is a new middle of countries—middle-income countries—which face weakening growth prospects due to stalled industrialization and premature deindustrialization. There is also the new middle comprising people who through industrialization have been lifted above absolute poverty when measured at low poverty lines. However, they are best described as precariat class because they are at risk of falling back into poverty due to the growth slow-downs that deindustrialization and premature deindustrialization are likely to engender.

The fourth stylized fact is that a new form of late economic development is emerging. Rather than industrialization of developing countries, there is a process of stalled industrialization, deindustrialization, and tertiarization.

The fifth stylized fact is that these processes will exacerbate global inequality in both components; the between-country as well as the within-country component. This is because on the one hand, stalled industrialization and deindustrialization will lead to slower economic growth and thus exacerbate the between-country component. On the other hand, the processes will also cause immiserizing growth with weak modern/formal sector employment generation potential, which in turn will lead to an exacerbation of within-country inequality.

A sixth stylized fact is that premature deindustrialization is evident in the data that capture only formal manufacturing or the Lewisian modern/GVC-integrated sector. This means that it is possible to argue that premature deindustrialization is a phenomenon occurring in the formal manufacturing or GVC/modern manufacturing sector. As deindustrialization occurs, workers move to informal, low-productivity manufacturing or services. The former—informal manufacturing—is akin to what Lewis (1979) referred to as the 'in-between sector'. This sector is likely to have lower productivity and lower wages than the modern, GVC-integrated sector and acts as a 'sponge' sector, absorbing workers at least temporarily.

A seventh stylized fact is that the new form of late economic development, driven by the fragmentation of global production into a GVC world, has changed the meaning of economic development to industrialization without—paradoxically—building entire industries.

The eighth stylized fact is that GVC participation has driven stalled industrialization and premature deindustrialization and ultimately weakened economic growth prospects for MICs as global production has spread thinner and thinner. The optimistic view is that it is no longer necessary to develop entire industries, as countries may specialize in particular stages of production and simply slot into GVCs where they can develop suppliers. The less optimistic perspective for developing countries is that higher-value-added tasks are located at the beginning and end stages of GVCs, whereas much developing country activity is around lower-value-adding assembly tasks in the middle of the 'smile curve'.

A ninth stylized fact is that there is a non-linear relationship between GVC participation and economic progress in that GVCs may help initially with growth in productivity but long-run development may be stunted, especially so if technology reduces the demand for abundant unskilled labour in developing countries. Furthermore, employment growth turns negative at productivity levels that are characteristic of middle-income countries.

Finally, a tenth stylized fact is that GVC-driven stalled industrialization and deindustrialization in MICs have also impact on the within-country component of global inequality by squeezing the labour share of the functional distribution of income and weakening employment growth. GVC participation is strongly associated to the squeeze of the labour share, which in turn has a strong association with rising pressure on within-country gross income inequality.

In sum, it is these ten stylized facts that form the golden thread of this book. Specifically, that there is a causal link between the emergence of a GVC world, stalled industrialization and premature deindustrialization, and rising global income inequality between and within countries.

6.4 Looking Ahead: Late Development, New Developmentalism, and Automation

6.4.1 The Question of Late Development

The central question for late development and developing countries ahead is whether modern services—tradeable, high-productivity services—can ever replace the potential of manufacturing for economic development and large-scale employment generation. An optimistic view is illustrated by Page (2012) who has argued that modern services such as tourism, IT, and finance or 'industries without smokestacks' and modern, high-tech agriculture have many of the features of manufacturing. For example, they are tradeable and connected to GVCs, have economies of scale, and are technologically dynamic (see also, Ghani and O'Connell, 2014) and indeed driven by recent technological change. Baldwin and Forslid (2020, pp. 2, 26) discuss how success in developing tradeable services require quite different strategies and 'mindsets' than developing manufacturing. They situate the rise of tradeable services and shift of those services from OECD to developing countries in the history of economic development thus:

> A first transformation shifted people from farms to factories and it was driven by mechanization. The second transformation shifted people from factories to offices and it was driven by computerization. The third…has yet to happen, so its impact on jobs is harder to encapsulate; it is driven by machine learning and communication technologies…If the automation of manufacturing means localized, jobless manufacturing, then many national development strategies will need rethinking. The changes may not appear for 10 or 20 years, but this is in line with the timeline of most national industrialization strategies, and so looking ahead is of vital importance.

This challenge to the future of manufacturing in economic development is echoed by Hallward-Driemeier and Nayyar (2017), Loungani et al. (2017), and World Bank (2017). Other services, however—such as retail and personal services—are non-tradeable and do not exhibit high levels of productivity nor innovation typically.

The rosy view is that of Ghani and O'Connell (2014) who argue that services are increasingly traded, linked to GVCs, and are able to generate large-scale employment. Ghani and Kharas (2010) compare China and India, noting India's services-led economic development, and that the potential market for tradeable services is large and not fully exploited to date.

In contrast, a less rosy view is illustrated by Rodrik (2018) who notes the heterogeneity of services. Even if it is the case that tourism, IT, and finance are highly tradeable and technologically dynamic like manufacturing, few of these sectors can generate large-scale employment for low-skilled workers while the employment generated in finance or business services is likely to be limited and largely for high-skilled labour. The sectors of personal and retail services are non-tradeable, technologically stagnant, and usually overwhelmingly occupied by informal, low-productivity, small firms. Rodrik (2018) compares labour productivity growth and employment generation in wholesale and retail trade as well as in personal and community services. He finds a negative correlation in the sense that sectors with the best productivity shed labour and vice versa. De Vries' (2019) empirical study broadens the concept of modern sectors to include modern agriculture, finance, and business services. The study finds premature deindustrialization is not apparent for modern sectors' output shares but is evident for employment shares. In short, modern agriculture and modern services might at best mitigate the premature deindustrialization of value-added though not the premature deindustrialization of employment. Modern agriculture and modern services cannot replace the loss of manufacturing jobs.

An alternative perspective is that services, rather than leading to a 'leapfrogging' of manufacturing, can also be seen as a complement to manufacturing. Kaldor (1968, p. 387) argued that services are 'derived from...industrial activities'. The question then is whether services are a leading complement or a lagging complement to manufacturing. Chang (2011) represents the latter view arguing that the most dynamic services are dependent on manufacturing. Dasgupta and Singh (2005, 2006) suggest that services can be leading, again drawing on India and IT. Furthermore, there is a debate on the extent to which the divide between manufacturing and services is blurring due to what Vandermerwe and Rada (1988) refer to as 'servitization'. This phenomenon has been observed in developed and developing countries (Neely et al., 2011) and refers to manufacturing firms not only having service activity for their own uses but also to sell to others. All of this discussion thus far suggests stalled industrialization and premature deindustrialization raise some big questions ahead related to whether service sector-led growth can generate sufficient and well-paid employment as well as value-added in developing countries.

So, what should developing countries do? In the mid-1970s Furtado (2020 [1974], p. 62) outlined three points on a spectrum of 'options for peripheral countries'. Specifically, he posited:

[a]t one extreme is sketched the possibility of the persistence of the tendencies... towards intense concentration of income for the benefit of a reduced minority. In the centre, there is the strengthening of the bureaucracies that control peripheral States...and the expansion of the privileged minority, to the detriment of the system's center. At the other extreme, there arises the possibility of fundamental political changes, under the pressure of the growing masses who are excluded from the fruits of development, which would move towards effecting substantive changes in the orientation of the development process.

Four decades on, developing countries face a spectrum of options and each with consequences for global inequality and trade-offs like Furtado's options in the 1970s. One strategic option is that developing countries simply continue on the GVC treadmill and try to make it work for industrialization. The empirical evidence in this book argues that this will be tough. That said, perhaps a small set of individual countries may achieve progress depending on industrial policy and their existing position in GVCs or the position in GVCs they are able to move to if they can control those entry points to GVCs over other countries. Kaplinsky and Morris (2016) argue that what developing countries need to do is to 'thin' or 'thicken' to capture rents through generating barriers to entry. They argue whether GVC participation leads to positive or negative outcomes depends on the capacity to generate, exploit, appropriate, or protect rents—in short, to protect activities that are in demand from competition through barriers to entry. Thus, rent boosting policies in manufacturing (in fragmented or 'vertically specialized GVCs') should be 'thinning', meaning specialization in order to gain a global competitive advantage. Only when this has been achieved should countries move to 'stretching', which is looking for higher rent niches; in doing so countries are seeking to avoid highly competitive chain segments.[1] In short, although on average the pattern is stalled industrialization and premature deindustrialization, it is possible that a country or a small set of countries could buck the broader trend by dominating and capturing enough value-added and

---

[1] In contrast, rent boosting policies in resource-based sectors (immobile or 'additive GVCs') should be 'thickening' or developing linkages with the local economy and increasing local value-added via content requirements and/or export taxes to ensure local content (subject to WTO rules) as well as skills and infrastructure development to ensure capture of sequential linkages in the chain by local companies.

employment at the expense of other developing countries and then seeking to reduce competition by raising barriers to entry.

If not, then there are three other options for developing countries in what is a 'tertiary trilemma', in the sense that it is based on three choices vis-à-vis the tertiary sector, and whether to support it or not in policies. Each entails trade-offs like Furtado's options in the 1970s. Developing countries face a choice between three strategies for late economic development that produce economic growth and employment growth. Those choices are as follows: The first option is the strategic promotion of higher-value-added services, meaning support through policies and subsidies of higher-value-added services such as finance, insurance, real-estate services, and business services that are tradeable internationally in keeping with Page's (2012) view of modern services to benefit from Baldwin's (2019) third 'unbundling'. State involvement could mean supporting such services through national development of commercial banks, and national financial institutions, for example. Or through direct or partial ownership and other forms of state capitalism in higher-value-added services and other modern services in order to help with international tradability in terms of competition with international competitors. This would be an externally orientated developmental state for high-value-added services. This is thus a strategy to pursue the Lewisian modern tertiary sector with vigour through expanding the state support to higher-value-added services-led growth and services that are tradeable. This could be based around the financial and business service sectors but expanded to include Page's (2012) 'industries without smokestacks' such as IT, tourism, and modern agriculture. This could generate much value-added if successful, though it has weak employment growth potential for low-skilled workers given the nature of these services. This option is thus likely unequalizing and may increase social tensions, as it would mean immiserizing growth for many—weak formal/modern sector employment growth for low-skilled workers—since only a minority of the population will be working in such high-value-added services. Plausibly, governments could redistribute the value-added generated through taxation, transfers, and public goods, though the politics of this would be challenging in the sense that financial sector interest groups would become dominant and may resist such redistributory policies.

A second option for developing countries is to pursue a late economic development strategy of state capitalism via state-owned enterprises (SOEs) based on expanding the share of lower-value-added services (potentially, alongside nationally-orientated manufacturing for a domestic market) by nationalization or subsidization of trade, catering, and hospitality; transport and storage; communication; government services; and community, social, and personal services. This would be a domestically orientated developmental state for lower productivity services, many of which are socially important services in terms of employment and public goods. This might be an approach Furtado would have been sympathetic to in light of the evident focus on services needed by the mass domestic market.[2] As noted, these sectors have higher potential for employment growth for low-skilled workers, albeit often in informal, low-wage services which could be formalized and wages raised for example. The constraint is such services have limited value-added potential. Thus, the support of these kinds of services would be a political decision to have an employment-led growth as far as is plausible in such services. A challenge will be the balance of payments constraint which could weigh heavily on such a strategy.

A third option is that governments of developing countries could—and many appear to be trying already—make a strategic choice to pursue a re-industrialization-led growth (and thus implicitly neglect services in relative terms at least through policy choices) through SOEs entering GVCs and/or subsidies to private exporting companies to join GVCs. There is some overlap with the strategy of trying to make GVC world work for economic development, albeit shallow economic development. The difference is rather than a relatively small set of internationally competitive companies entering GVCs, the third option of the trilemma is an externally orientated developmental state for GVC manufacturing. The state would lead negotiations with TNCs, shape conditions in which a country joins a GVC (as far as the country has some negotiating power, for example in exchange for access to the domestic consumer market if of reasonable size), and potentially follow the traditional or new set of developmental state policies, such as directed finance and low or negative interest rates. State support would need to navigate or circumnavigate World Trade Organization (WTO) rules. This option thus requires state activism in the form of direct or indirect subsidies to SOEs and domestic private companies to become GVC suppliers (i.e. through subsidized or directed credit, protection, and/or upskilling labour force) and/or incentives to attract international companies as direct foreign investors (i.e. through fiscal subsidies, tax breaks, or other incentives). The challenge with this state-led re-industrialization is that it is predicated

---

[2] Furtado, it should be noted, did not call for isolationism. Instead, 'the strategic aim becomes the need to minimize the cost of dependence and to explore all paths leading to real interdependence. This involves changing the power relationships underlying the international economic order. The struggle against dependence thus requires an effort to change the global configuration of the system' (1983b [1978], p. 7).

on participation in the very part of the global economy, GVCs, that has engendered stalled industrialization and deindustrialization in many MICs so far. It is thus an open question as to whether a state capitalist- or SOE-dominated approach can provide more employment-led growth and avoid deindustrialization in a GVC world.

It is clear that each of these choices is suboptimal and involves trade-offs for value-added, employment growth, and real wages for different types of workers. Adding to the struggle for development is the likelihood that technological change will accelerate deindustrialization of employment because the kinds of jobs common in developing countries—such as routine manufacturing work—are substantially more susceptible to automation. If more manufacturing jobs are automated, workers will continue to move into the service sector, leading to a bloating of service sector employment and wage stagnation, especially so in informal services. Furthermore, as noted in the introductory chapter, the COVID-19 pandemic is likely to act as a super-accelerator of technological trends. The process of stalled industrialization, deindustrialization, and tertiarization may gain speed as the mobility of some service sector jobs becomes evident through home working in OECD countries. Jobs may move to countries, especially countries with an English-speaking workforce, and the process of Baldwin's (2020b) 'tele-migrating' may become more evident in developing countries.

6.4.2   Industrialization, Deindustrialization, and Developmentalism in Developing Countries

In the previous discussion, it was noted that many middle-income developing countries are already pursuing some kind of re-industrialization strategy through state capitalism or a 'new developmentalism'. New developmentalism is characterized by the use of SOEs for economic development purposes. Furthermore, a substantial domestic protectionism is re-emerging, which is subtler in its statism than the classical developmentalism of the 1960s/70s (see Aggarwal and Evenett, 2010; Wade, 2011). As Musacchio and Lazzarini (2014) show, many developing countries' governments have retained ownership in entirety or part-ownership via 'golden shares' in part-privatized SOEs. Even if the ownership of SOEs is minority rather than majority ownership, it is suffi-cient to ensure that the state remains the largest single investor, and thus shapes the direction of the enterprise. Thus, the state can still act strategically. In short, a new kind of developmentalism is possible and already emerging.

This new developmentalism is largely focused on catch-up strategies (see Ban, 2013; Bresser-Pereira, 2011), although there is also a 'social developmentalism' which is concerned with domestic demand generation through income redistribution, wage rises, and combining growth with redistribution (see Amado and Mollo, 2015). However, the success of new developmentalism in economic development terms is very much dependent on commodity prices and/or low-interest rates for financing and the policy space that opened in the late 2000s following the post-global financial crisis. There is the issue too of the suboptimal insertion of SOEs into GVC entry points where activities are less profitable, and thus the risk of simply subsidizing inputs to TNCs. Consequently, it is unclear whether the trend towards a developmental state Mark II or a new developmentalism will lead to substantial and genuine economic development for developing countries in the long run.

6.4.3 Industrialization, Deindustrialization, and Automation

One final issue looking ahead, already noted above in passing, is that of the 'fourth industrial revolution' or automation, which is likely to quicken the pace in the years ahead in the GVC-integrated, Lewisian modern sector of manufacturing. Stalled industrialization and premature deindustrialization of employment could simply mean an industrialization with weaker employment growth. In the forthcoming years, a range of new technologies is likely to have profound impacts on work and wages in developed as well as developing countries. Many jobs in developing countries—such as routine manufacturing work—are susceptible to this automation of production. However, rather than causing mass unemployment, artificial intelligence and robots are more likely to lead to stagnant wages and to further exacerbate the deindustrialization of employment in the developing world. In a sense there is a 'new reserve army of labour' type-argument as a result of automation (see discussion of Schlogl and Sumner, 2020).

If manufacturing jobs are automated, workers will flood into the service sector, driving down wages. This will likely put upward pressure on national inequality, potentially placing the existing social contract under strain. It is a crucial question how middle-income developing countries should respond in terms of public policy. With a view to the Lewis model of economic development, automation will create unlimited supplies of artificial labour or a 'robot reserve army' in the GVC-integrated sector. Automation will challenge the competitive advantage of low-cost labour of late developers, and stalled industrialization and premature deindustrialization will likely worsen as a result.

6.5 Conclusions

In conclusion, this book has presented a production-based theory of global inequality and its persistence. The main aspects of this theory are as follows: First, paradoxically, there is prematurity within lateness (of economic development). Global inequality persists due to the limitations on developing countries' catch-up as a result of stalled industrialization and premature deindustrialization. Second, there is a shallowness (of late economic development). Global inequality persists as deep industrialization has been disembedded from the idea of economic development. Third, consequentially, there is a stuntedness (of late economic development). Global inequality persists as deep industrialization has been replaced with a shallow form of industrialization of a relatively small number of domestic companies slotting into tasks within GVCs. Fourth, there is immiseration in terms of growth. Global inequality persists because the resulting growth squeezes the labour share and puts pressure on gross income inequality, leading to weaker modern sector employment growth. Consequently, labour shifts to lower-paid and less equal informal manufacturing or informal services. This production-based theory of global inequality explains both the between- and within-country inequality component of global inequality. The theory helps to explain how the set of the four great transformations outlined in this book can result in prematurity, shallowness, stuntedness, and immiseration and ultimately the persistence of global inequality. In short, diminished development.

A final thought: What would Furtado, or for that matter, Lewis, Kaldor, or Kuznets make of the contemporary economic development prospects for developing countries if they were alive today? They would have been surprised about the persistence of economic dualism so many years after their writings; surprised, no doubt that tertiarization had become the default pathway for many developing countries; and taken aback by the fact that the very idea of deep industrialization had shrunk to specialization in a limited set of production tasks in a GVC world. In addition, it is certain that they would advocate further investigation of the role of the state in late economic development. The intention of this book is for it to serve as a new impulse on the study of structural transformation; the different paths of late economic development that developing countries experience today; and on the implications of these different paths for economic growth, inequality, and employment.

References

Acemoglu, D., & Autor, D. H. (2011). Skills, Tasks and Technologies: Implications for Employment and Earnings. In: O. Ashenfelter & D. Card (eds), *Handbook of Labor Economics, Vol. 4*, pp. 1043–1171. Amsterdam: Elsevier.

Acemoglu, D., & Robinson J. A. (2002). The Political Economy of the Kuznets Curve. *Review of Development Economics, 6*(2), 183–203.

Adams, R. H. Jr. (2004). Economic Growth, Inequality and Poverty: Estimating the Growth Elasticity of Poverty. *World Development, 32*(11), 1989–2014.

Adermon, A., & Gustavsson, M. (2015). Job Polarization and Task-Biased Technological Change: Evidence from Sweden, 1975–2005. *The Scandinavian Journal of Economics, 117*(3), 878–917.

Aggarwal, V. K., & Evenett, S. J. (2010). Financial Crisis, 'New' Industrial Policy, and the Bite of Multilateral Trade Rules. *Asian Economic Policy Review, 5*, 221–44.

Agostino, M., Giunta, A., Nugent, J. B., Scalera, D., & Trivieri, F. (2015). The Importance of Being a Capable Supplier: Italian Industrial Firms in Global Value Chains. *International Small Business Journal: Researching Entrepreneurship, 33*(7), 708–30.

Alderson, A. S. (1999). Explaining Deindustrialization: Globalization, Failure, or Success? *American Sociological Review, 64*(5), 701–21.

Amado, A. M., & Mollo, M. (2015). The 'developmentalism' debate in Brazil: Some economic and political issues. *Review of Keynesian Economics, 3*(1), 77–89.

Amirapu, A., & Subramanian, A. (2015). Manufacturing or Services? An Indian Illustration of a Development Dilemma. *CGD Working Paper 408*. Washington, DC: Center for Global Development.

Amsden, A. (1989). *Asia's Next Giant: South Korea and Late Industrialization.* New York City, NY: Oxford University Press.

Amsden, A. (2001). *The Rise of 'The Rest': Challenges to the West from Late-Industrializing Economies.* Oxford: Oxford University Press.

Anand, S., & Segal, P. (2015). The Global Distribution of Income. In: A. B. Atkinson & F. Bourguignon (eds), *Handbook of Income Distribution Vol. 2*, pp. 937–79. Amsterdam: Elsevier.

Anand, S., & Segal, P. (2017). Who Are the Global Top 1%? *World Development, 95*, 111–26.

Angeles, L. (2010). An Alternative Test of Kuznets' Hypothesis. *The Journal of Economic Inequality, 8*, 463–73.

Arrighi, G. (1990). The Developmentalist Illusion: A Reconceptualization of the Semiperiphery. In: W. G. Martin (ed.), *Semiperipheral States in the World-Economy*, pp. 11–42. Westport, CT: Greenwood Press.

Atolia, M., Loungani, P., Marquis, M., & Papageorgiou, C. (2020). Rethinking Development Policy: What Remains of Structural Transformation? *World Development*, Elsevier, *128*(C).

Autor, D. H., & Dorn, D. (2013). The Growth of Low-Skill Service Jobs and the Polarization of the US Labor Market. *The American Economic Review, 103*(5), 1553–97.

Autor, D. H., Levy, F., & Murnane, R. J. (2003). The Skill Content of Recent Technological Change: An Empirical Exploration. *The Quarterly Journal of Economics, 118*(4), 1279–1333.

Bacon, R. W., & Eltis, W. (1976). *Britain's Economic Problem: Too Few Producers.* London: Macmillan.

Baldwin, R. (2006). *Globalisation: The Great Unbundling(s)*. Helsinki: Economic Council of Finland.

Baldwin, R. (2016). *The Great Convergence: Information Technology and the New Globalization*. Cambridge, MA: The Belknap Press of Harvard University Press.

Baldwin, R. (2019). The Globotics Upheaval: Globalisation, Robotics and the Future of Work. New York: W and N.

Baldwin, R. (2020a, 22 March). The Supply Side Matters: Guns versus Butter, COVID-Style. *VOX CEPR Policy Portal*.

Baldwin, R. (2020b, 29 May). COVID, Hysteresis, and the Future of Work. *VOX CEPR Policy Portal*.

Baldwin, R. & Forslid, R. (2020). Globotics and Development: When Manufacturing Is Jobless and Services Are Tradable. National Bureau of Economic Research (NBER) Working Paper 26731. NBER: Cambridge, MA.

Baldwin, R. & Okubo, T. (2019). GVC Journeys: Industrialisation and Deindustrialisation in the Age of the Second Unbundling. *Journal of the Japanese and International Economies*, *52*, 53–67.

Baldwin, R., & Venables, A. J. (2013). Spiders and snakes: Offshoring and agglomeration in the global economy. *Journal of International Economics*, *90*(2), 245–54.

Ban, C. (2013). Brazil's Liberal Neo-developmentalism: New Paradigm or Edited Orthodoxy? *Review of International Political Economy*, *20*(2), 298–331.

Banga, K. (2016). Impact of Global Value Chains on Employment in India. *Journal of Economic Integration*, *31*(3), 631–73.

Barrientos, S., Gereffi, G., & Rossi, A. (2011). Economic and Social Upgrading in Global Production Networks: A New Paradigm for a Changing World. *International Labour Review*, *150*(3–4), 319–40.

Barrientos, S., Gereffi, G., & Pickles, J. (2016). New Dynamics of Upgrading in Global Value Chains: Shifting Terrain for Suppliers and Workers in the Global South. *Environment and Planning A: Economy and Space*, *48*(7), 1214–19.

Baymul, C., & Sen, K. (2020). Was Kuznets Right? New Evidence on the Relationship between Structural Transformation and Inequality. *The Journal of Development Studies*, 56(9), 1–20.

Bazen, S., & Thirlwall, A. P. (1986). De-Industrialization in the UK. In: B. Atkinson (ed.), *Developments in Economics No. 2*. Ormskirk: Causeway Press.

Bazen, S., & Thirlwall, A. P. (1989). Why Manufacturing Industry Matters. *Economic Affairs*, *9*(4), 8–10.

Bazen, S., & Thirlwall, A. P. (1992). *Deindustrialization (Studies in Economics and Business)*. Portsmouth, NH: Heinemann.

Bengtsson, E., & Waldenström, D. (2018). Capital Shares and Income Inequality: Evidence from the Long Run. *The Journal of Economic History*, *78*(3), 712–43.

Benkovskis, K., Masso, J., Tkacevs, O., Vahter, P., & Yashiro N. (2017). Export and Productivity in Global Value Chains: Comparative Evidence from Latvia and Estonia. *OECD Economics Department Working Papers 1448*. Paris: OECD Publishing.

Berman, E., Bound, J., & Griliches, Z. (1994). Changes in the Demand for Skilled Labor within U.S. Manufacturing: Evidence from the Annual Survey of Manufacturers. *The Quarterly Journal of Economics*, *109*(2), 367–97.

Berman, E., Bound, J., & Machin, S. (1998). Implications of Skill-Biased Technological Change: International Evidence. *The Quarterly Journal of Economics*, *113*(4), 1245–79.

Bernhardt, T., & Pollak, R. (2016). Economic and Social Upgrading Dynamics in Global Manufacturing Value Chains: A Comparative Analysis. *Environment and Planning A: Economy and Space*, *48*(7), 1220–43.

Blair, J. (2017). Contextualising Compliance: Hybrid Governance in Global Value Chains. *New Political Economy*, *22*(2), 169–85.

Bluestone, B., & Harrison, B. (1982). *The Deindustrialization of America*. New York City, NY: Basic Books.

Boianovsky, M. (2007). A View from the Tropics: Celso Furtado and the Theory of Economic Development in the 1950s. *History of Political Economy, 42*(2), 221–66.

Bresser-Pereira, L. C. (2011). From Old to New Developmentalism in Latin America. In: J. O. Ocampo & J. Ross (eds), *The Oxford Handbook of Latin American Economics*, pp. 108–29. Oxford: Oxford University Press.

Brynjolfsson, E., & McAfee, A. (2014). *The Second Machine Age: Work, Progress, and Prosperity in a Time of Brilliant Technologies*. New York City, NY: W. W. Norton & Co.

Budd, J. W., Konings, J., & Slaughter, M. J. (2005). Wages and International Rent Sharing in Multinational Firms. *The Review of Economics and Statistics, 87*(1), 73–84.

Cáceres, L. R. (2017). Deindustrialization and Economic Stagnation in El Salvador. *CEPAL Review, 122*, 57–77.

Cairncross, A. (1979). What Is Deindustrialisation? In: F. Blackaby (ed.), *De-Industrialisation*. London: Heinemann Educational Books.

Cantore, N., Clara, M., Lavopa, A., & Soare, C. (2017). Manufacturing as an Engine of Growth: Which is the Best Fuel? *Structural Change and Economic Dynamics, 42*, 56–66.

Caraballo, J., & Jiang X. (2016). Value-Added Erosion in Global Value Chains: An Empirical Assessment. *Journal of Economic Issues, 50*(1), 288–96.

Card, D. E., & DiNardo, J. E. (2002). Skill-Biased Technological Change and Rising Wage Inequality: Some Problems and Puzzles. *Journal of Labor Economics, 20*(4), 733–83.

Cardoso, F. H. and Faletto, E. (1979). *Dependency and Development in Latin America*. Berkeley and Los Angeles, CA: University of California Press.

Casella, B., Bolwijn, R., Moran, D., & Kanemoto, K. (2019). Improving the Analysis of Global Value Chains: The UNCTAD-Eora Database. *Transnational Corporations* 26(3), 115–142.

Cavalcanti, T. V., Mohaddes, K., & Raissi, M. (2015). Commodity Price Volatility and the Sources of Growth. *Journal of Applied Econometrics, 30*(6), 857–73.

Chang, H.-J. (1994). *The Political Economy of Industrial Policy*. London and Basingstoke: Macmillan.

Chang, H.-J. (2002). Kicking Away the Ladder: Development Strategy in Historical Perspective. Anthem Press: New York.

Chang, H.J. (2011). 23 Things They Don't Tell You About Capitalism. Allen Lane (Penguin): London.

Chen, X. (2011). Increasing Returns to Scale in US Manufacturing Industries: Evidence from Direct and Reverse Regression. *Bureau d'Economie Théorique et Appliquée (BETA) Working Paper 2011-11*. Strasbourg: UDS.

Chenery, H. B. (1960). Patterns of Industrial Growth. *The American Economic Review, 50*(4), 624–54.

Chenery, H. B. (1975). The Structuralist Approach to Development Policy. *The American Economic Review, 65*(2), 310–16.

Chenery, H. B. (1979). *Structural Change and Development Policy*. New York City, NY: Oxford University Press.

Chenery, H. B., & Syrquin, M. (1975). *Patterns of Development 1950–1970*. Washington, DC: World Bank.

Chenery, H. B., Robinson, S., & Syrquin, M. (1986). *Industrialization and Growth: A Comparative Study*. Washington, DC: World Bank.

Clark, C. (1940). *The Conditions of Economic Progress*. New York: Macmillan Company.

Coe, N., & Yeung, H. W.-C. (2019). Global Production Networks: Mapping Recent Conceptual Developments. *Journal of Economic Geography, 19*(4), 775–801.

Cowen, T. (2013). *Average Is Over: Powering America beyond the Age of the Great Stagnation*. New York City, NY: Penguin Group.

Cruz, M. (2014). Premature De-Industrialization: Theory, Evidence and Policy Recommendations in the Mexican Case. *Cambridge Journal of Economics, 39*(1), 113–37.

Cypher, J. M. (2015). Emerging Contradictions of Brazil's Neo-Developmentalism: Precarious Growth, Redistribution, and Deindustrialization. *Journal of Economic Issues, 49*(3), 617–48.

Dao, M. C., Das, M., Koczan, Z., & Lian, W. (2017a). Why Is Labor Receiving a Smaller Share of Global Income? Theory and Empirical Evidence. *IMF Working Paper 17/169*. Washington DC: International Monetary Fund.

Dao, M. C., Das, M., Koczan, Z., & Lian, W. (2017b, 8 September). Routinisation, Globalisation, and the Fall in Labour's Share of Income. *VOX CEPR Policy Portal*.

Das, M. (2018). Does the Exposure to Routinization Explain the Evolution of the Labour Share of Income? Evidence from Asia. *ADBI Working Paper No. 901*. Tokyo: Asian Development Bank Institute.

Das, M., & Hilgenstock, B. (2018). The Exposure to Routinization: Labor Market Implications for Developed and Developing Economies. *IMF Working Paper No. 18/135*. Washington, DC: International Monetary Fund.

Dasgupta, S., & Singh, A. (2005). Will Services be the New Engine of Indian Economic Growth? *Development and Change, 36*(6), 1035–57.

Dasgupta, S., & Singh, A. (2006). Manufacturing, Services and Premature Deindustrialization in Developing Countries: A Kaldorian Analysis. *UNU-WIDER Research Working Paper 49/2006*. Helsinki: United Nations University World Institute for Development Economics Research.

Daudey, E., & Garcia-Penalosa, C. (2007). The Personal and the Factor Distributions of Income in a Cross-Section of Countries. *Journal of Development Studies, 43*(5), 812–29.

David, H., & Dorn, D. (2013). The Growth of Low-Skill Service Jobs and the Polarization of the US Labor Market. *American Economic Review, 103*(5), 1553–97.

DeGroot, H. L. (2000). *Growth, Unemployment, and Deindustrialization*. Cheltenham: Edward Elgar Publishing.

DeVries, G. (2019). Premature Deindustrialization? A Reappraisal. Paper prepared for 'The Future of Industrial Work: New Pathways and Policies of Structural Transformation', UNIDO/GPID/UNU-MERIT workshop, Vienna, 19–20 September.

Dean, J., Fung, K. C., & Wang, Z. (2007). Measuring the Vertical Specialization in Chinese Trade. *Office of Economics Working Paper No. 2007-01-A*. Washington, DC: US International Trade Commission.

Dedrick, J., Kraemer, K. L., & Linden, G. (2010). Who Profits from Innovation in Global Value Chains? A Study of the iPod and Notebook PCs. *Industrial and Corporate Change, 19*(1), 81–116.

DelPrete, D., Giovannetti, G., & Marvasi, E. (2017). Global Value Chains Participation and Productivity Gains for North African Firms. *Review of World Economics, 153*(4), 675–701.

Diao, X., & McMillan, M. (2018). Toward an Understanding of Economic Growth in Africa: A Reinterpretation of the Lewis Model. *World Development, 109*, 511–22.

Diao, X., McMillan, M., & Rodrik, D. (2017). The Recent Growth Boom in Developing Economies: A Structural-Change Perspective. *NBER Working Paper No. 23132*. Cambridge, MA: National Bureau of Economic Research.

Díaz-Mora, C., Gandoy, R., & Gonzalez-Diaz, B. (2018). Strengthening the Stability of Exports through GVC Participation: The Who and How Matters. *Journal of Economic Studies, 45*(3), 610–37.

Dollar, D., & Kraay, A. (2002). Growth Is Good for the Poor. *Journal of Economic Growth, 7*, 195–225.

Dollar, D., Kleineberg, T., and Kraay, A. (2013). Growth Still Is Good for the Poor. *World Bank Policy Research Working Paper No. 6568*. Washington, DC: World Bank.

Donaldson, J. A. (2008). Growth Is Good for Whom, When, How? Economic Growth and Poverty Reduction in Exceptional Cases. *World Development, 36*(11), 2127–43.

DosSantos, T. (1970). The Structure of Dependence. *American Economic Review, 60*(2), 231–6.

Duarte, M., & Restuccia, D. (2010). The Role of the Structural Transformation in Aggregate Productivity. *The Quarterly Journal of Economics, 125*(1), 129–73.

Edward, P., & Sumner, A. (2018). Global Poverty and Inequality: Are the Revised Estimates Open to an Alternative Interpretation? *Third World Quarterly, 39*(3), 487–509.

Edward, P., & Sumner, A. (2019). *The End of Poverty: Inequality and Growth in Global Perspective.* London: Palgrave Macmillan.

Elsby, M. W., Hobijn, B., & Şahin, A. (2013). The Decline of the US Labor Share. *Brookings Papers on Economic Activity, 2013*(2), 1–63.

Emmanuel, A. (1972). *Unequal Exchange: A Study of the Imperialism of Trade.* New York and London: Monthly Review Press.

Erauskin, I. (2020). The Labor Share and Income Inequality: Some Empirical Evidence for the Period 1990–2015. *Applied Economic Analysis* (ahead of print).

Feenstra, R. C., Inklaar, R., & Timmer, M. P. (2015). The Next Generation of the Penn World Table. *American Economic Review, 105*(10), 3150–82.

Fei, J. C. H., & Ranis, G. (1964). *Development of the Labor Surplus Economy: Theory and Policy.* Homewood IL: Richard A. Irwin.

Felipe, J., Kumar, U., & Abdon, A. (2014). How Rich Countries Became Rich and Why Poor Countries Remain Poor: It's the Economic Structure…Duh! *Japan & the World Economy, 29*, 46–58.

Felipe, J., & Mehta, A. (2016). *Deindustrialization? A Global Perspective.* Economics Letters, 149(C), 148–51.

Felipe, J., Mehta, A., & Rhee, C. (2018). Manufacturing Matters…But it's the Jobs that Count. *Cambridge Journal of Economics, 43*(1), 139–68.

Felman, J., Sandefur, J., Subramanian, A., & Duggan, J. (2019, December 9). Is India's Consumption Really Falling? *Center for Global Development Blog.*

Ferreira, F., & Sánchez-Páramo, C. (2017, October 13). A richer array of international poverty lines. World Bank Blogs.

Fischer, A. (2011). Beware the Fallacy of Productivity Reductionism. *The European Journal of Development Research, 23*(4), 521–6.

Fischer, A. M. (2014). The Social Value of Employment and the Redistributive Imperative for Development. *UNDP Human Development Report Office, Occasional Paper.* New York City, NY: United Nations Development Programme.

Fischer, A. M. (2018). *Poverty as Ideology: Rescuing Social Justice from Global Development Agendas.* Zed Books: London.

Fontagné, L., & Harrison, A.E. (2017). The Factory-Free Economy: Outsourcing, Servitization, and the Future of Industry. *NBER Working Paper 23016.* Cambridge, MA: National Bureau of Economic Research.

Formai, S., & Vergara Caffarelli, F. (2016). Quantifying the Productivity Effects of Global Sourcing. *Bank of Italy Temi di Discussione (Working Paper) No. 1075.* Rome: Bank of Italy.

Fouré, J., Bénassy-Quéré, A., & Fontagné, L. (2012). The Great Shift: Macroeconomic Projections for the World Economy at the 2050 Horizon. *CEPII Working Paper 2012-03.* Paris: CEPII.

Frank, A. G. (1966). The Development of Underdevelopment. *Monthly Review, 18*(4), 17–31.

Frank, A. G. (1972). *Lumpenbourgeoisie: Lumpen Development, Dependence, Class and Politics in Latin America.* New York City, NY: Monthly Review Press.

Fransen, L., & Burgoon, B. (2012). A Market for Worker Rights: Explaining Business Support for International Private Labour Regulation. *Review of International Political Economy, 19*(2), 236–66.

Frenkel, R., & Rapetti, M. (2012). External Fragility or Deindustrialization: What Is the Main Threat to Latin American Countries in the 2010s? *World Social and Economic Review*, *1*, 37–57.

Furtado, C. (1954 [1952]). The Formation of Capital and Economic Development. Revista Brasileira de Economia, 6(3), 7–46.

Furtado, C. (1957). A analise marginalista e a teoria do subdesenvolvimento. In: Contribuições a Analise do Desenvolvimento Econômico—Escritos em Homenagem a Eugenio Gudin, 163–75. Rio de Janeiro: Agir.

Furtado, C. (1958). The External Disequilibrium in the Underdeveloped Economies. Indian *Journal of Economics*, *38*(151), 403–10.

Furtado, C. (1963). *The Economic Growth of Brazil: A Survey from Colonial to Modern Times*. Los Angeles: University of California Press.

Furtado, C. (1964 [1961]). *Development and Underdevelopment*. Berkeley, CA: University of California Press.

Furtado, C. (1965). Development and Stagnation in Latin America: A Structuralist Approach. *Studies in Comparative International Development*, *1*, 159–75.

Furtado, C. (1969). Formação econômica da América Latina. RJ, Lia Editora.

Furtado, C. (1970a). *Economic Development of Latin America: A Survey from Colonial Times to the Cuban Revolution*. Cambridge: Cambridge University Press.

Furtado, C. (1970b). *Obstacles to Development in Latin America*. New York: Anchor Books-Doubleday.

Furtado, C. (1973). Elements of a Theory of Underdevelopment: The Underdeveloped Structures. In: H. Bernstein (ed.), *Underdevelopment and Development: The Third World Today*, pp. 33–43. Harmondsworth: Penguin Books.

Furtado, C. (1983a). *Breve introducción al desarrollo: Un enfoque interdisciplinario* (Brief Introduction to Development: An Interdisciplinary Approach). (1st Portuguese ed., 1980.) Mexico: Siglo XXI Editores.

Furtado, C. (1983b [1978]). *Accumulation and Development: The Logic of Industrial Civilization*. Oxford: Martin Robertson.

Furtado, C. (2009 [1998]). *Global Capitalism*. Ciudad de México: Fondo de Cultura Economica.

Furtado, C. (2020a [1974]). *The Myth of Economic Development*. Polity Books.

Furtado, C. (2020b). The Myth of Economic Development and the Future of the Third World. *Review of Political Economy* 33(1), 16–27.

Galbraith, J. K. (2011). Inequality and Economic and Political Change: A Comparative Perspective. *Cambridge Journal of Regions, Economy and* Society, *4*(1), 13–27.

Galindo-Rueda, F., & Verger, F. (2016). OECD Taxonomy of Economic Activities Based on R & D Intensity. *OECD Science, Technology and Industry Working Paper No. 2016/04*. Paris: OECD Publishing.

Gereffi, G. (1994). The Organization of Buyer-Driven Global Commodity Chains: How US Retailers Shape Overseas Production Networks. In: G. Gereffi & M. Korzeniewicz (eds), *Contributions in Economics and Economic History*, pp. 95–122. Westport, CT: Praeger.

Gereffi, G. (1999). International Trade and Industrial Upgrading in the Apparel Commodity Chain. *Journal of International Economics* 38, 37–70.

Gereffi, G. (2018). *Global Value Chains and Development: Redefining the Contours of 21st Century Capitalism*. Cambridge: Cambridge University Press.

Gerschenkron, A. (1962). *Economic Backwardness in Historical Perspective: A Book of Essays*. Cambridge, MA: Belknap Press of Harvard University Press.

Ghani, E., & Kharas, H. (2010). The Service Revolution. *Economic Premise*, *14*, 1–5.

Ghani, E., & O'Connell, S. D. (2014). *Can Service be a Growth Escalator in Low-Income Countries?* Washington, DC: The World Bank.

Gimet, C., Guilhon, B., & Roux, N. (2015). Social Upgrading in Globalized Production: The Case of the Textile and Clothing Industry. *International Labour Review, 154*(3), 303–27.

Giuliani, E., Pietrobelli, C., & Rabellotti, R. (2005). Upgrading in Global Value Chains: Lessons from Latin American Clusters. *World Development, 33*(4), 549–73.

Goldin, C. & Katz, L. F. (2009). *The Race between Education and Technology.* Cambridge, MA: Cambridge University Press.

Gollin, D. (2014). The Lewis Model: A 60-Year Retrospective. *Journal of Economic Perspectives, 28*(3), 71–88.

Gollin, D., Jedwab, R., & Vollrath, D. (2016). Urbanization With and Without Structural Transformation. *Journal of Economic Growth, 21*(1), 35–70.

Gollin, D., Lagakos, D., & Waugh, M. E. (2014). Agricultural Productivity Differences across Countries. *American Economic Review, 104*(5), 65–70.

Goos, M. (2018). The Impact of Technological Progress on Labour Markets: Policy Challenges. *Oxford Review of Economic Policy, 34*(3), 362–75.

Goos, M., & Manning, A. (2007). Lousy and Lovely Jobs: The Rising Polarization of Work in Britain. *The Review of Economics and Statistics, 89*(1), 118–33.

Goos, M., Manning, A., & Salomons, A. (2014). Explaining Job Polarization: Routine-Biased Technological Change and Offshoring. *American Economic Review, 104*(8), 2509–26.

Green, D. A., & Sand, B. M. (2015). Has the Canadian Labour Market Polarized? *Canadian Journal of Economics, 48*(2), 612–46.

Guerriero, M. (2019). Democracy and the Labor Share of Income: A Cross-Country Analysis. *ADBI Working Paper No. 919.* Tokyo: Asian Development Bank Institute.

Gwynne, R. N. (1986). The Deindustrialization of Chile, 1974–1984. *Bulletin of Latin America Research, 54*(1), 1–23.

Hallward-Driemeier, M., & Nayyar, G. (2017). *Trouble in the Making? The Future of Manufacturing-led Development.* Washington, DC: World Bank.

Hamid, N., & Khan, M. (2015). Pakistan: A Case of Premature Deindustrialization? *The Lahore Journal of Economics, 20*(4), 107–41.

Haraguchi, N., Cheng, C. F. C., & Smeets, E. (2017). The Importance of Manufacturing in Economic Development: Has this Changed? *World Development, 93*, 293–315.

Haraguchi, N., Martorano, B., & Sanfilippo, M. (2019). What Factors Drive Successful Industrialization? Evidence and Implications for Developing Countries. *Structural Change and Economic Dynamics, 49*, 266–76.

Harrigan, J., Reshef, A., & Toubal, F. (2016). The March of the Techies: Technology, Trade, and Job Polarization in France, 1994–2007. *NBER Working Paper No. 22110.* Cambridge, MA: National Bureau of Economic Research.

Harris, J. R., & Todaro, M. P. (1970). Migration, Unemployment and Development: A Two-Sector Analysis. *American Economic Review, 60*, 126–42.

Hein, E., & Mundt, M. (2012). Financialisation and the Requirements and Potentials for Wage-Led Recovery: A Review Focusing on the G20. *Conditions of Work and Employment Series No. 37.* Geneva: International Labour Office.

Heintz, J. (2010). Employment, Economic Development and Poverty Reduction: Critical Issues and Policy Challenges. *UNRISD Flagship Report: Combating Poverty and Inequality.* Geneva: UNRISD.

Henderson, J., & Phillips, R. (2007). Unintended Consequences: Social Policy, State Institutions and the 'Stalling' of the Malaysian Industrialization Project. *Economy and Society, 36*(1), 78–102.

Herrendorf, B., Herrington, C., & Valentinyi, Á. (2015). Sectoral Technology and Structural Transformation. *American Economic Journal: Macroeconomics, 7*(4), 104–33.

Herrendorf, B., Rogerson, R., & Valentinyi, Á. (2013). Two Perspectives on Preferences and Structural Transformation. *American Economic Review, 103*(7), 2752–89.

Herrendorf, B., Rogerson, R., & Valentinyi, Á. (2014). Growth and Structural Transformation. In: P. Aghion & S. Durlauf (eds), *Handbook of Economic Growth, Vol. 2*, pp. 855–941. Amsterdam: Elsevier.

Hijzen, A., Martins, P. S., Schank, T., & Upward, R. (2013). Foreign-Owned Firms around the World: A Comparative Analysis of Wages and Employment at the Micro-Level. *European Economic Review, 60*, 170–88.

Hirschman, A. O. (1958). *The Strategy of Economic Development*. New Haven, CT: Yale University Press.

Hirschman, A. O. (1968). The Political Economy of Import-Substituting Industrialization in Latin America. *The Quarterly Journal of Economics, 82*(1), 1–32.

Hirschman, A. O. (1971). *A Bias for Hope*. New Haven, CT: Yale University Press.

Hogrefe, J., & Yao, Y. (2016). Offshoring and Labor Income Risk: An Empirical Investigation. *Empirical Economics, 50*(3), 1045–63.

Hummels, D., Ishii, J., & Yi, K.-M. (2001).The Nature of Growth of Vertical Specialization in World Trade. *Journal of International Economics, 54*(1), 75–96.

Humphrey, J., & Schmitz, H. (2002). How Does Insertion in Global Value Chains Affect Upgrading in Industrial Clusters? *Regional Studies, 36*(9), 1017–27.

IMF (2019). *World Economic Outlook Database*. Washington, DC. International Monetary Fund.

Ivarsson, I., & Alvstam, C. G. (2011). Upgrading in Global Value-Chains: A Case Study of Technology-Learning among IKEA-Suppliers in China and Southeast Asia. *Journal of Economic* Geography, *11*, 731–52.

Jenkins, R. (2015a). International Competitiveness in Manufacturing and the China Effect. In: J. Weiss & M. Tribe (eds), *Routledge Handbook of Industry and Development*. London: Routledge, 259–73.

Jenkins, R. (2015b). Is Chinese Competition Causing Deindustrialization in Brazil? *Latin American Perspectives, 42*(6), 42–63.

Johnson, C. (1982). *MITI and the Japanese Miracle: The Growth of Industrial Policy 1925–1975*. Stanford, CA: Stanford University Press.

Johnson, G. (1997). Changes in Earnings Inequality: The Role of Demand Shifts. *Journal of Economic Perspectives, 11*, 41–54.

Johnson, P., & Papageorgiou, C. (2020). What Remains of Cross-Country Convergence? *Journal of Economic Literature, 58*(1), 129–75.

Kaldor, N. (1956). Alternative Theories of Distribution. *The Review of Economic Studies, 23*(2), 83–100.

Kaldor, N. (1957). A Model of Economic Growth. *The Economic Journal, 67*(268), 591–624.

Kaldor, N. (1961). Capital Accumulation and Economic Growth. In: F. A. Lutz & D. C. Hague (eds), *The Theory of Capital*, pp. 177–222. London: Palgrave Macmillan.

Kaldor, N. (1966). Marginal Productivity and the Macro-Economic Theories of Distribution: Comment on Samuelson and Modigliani. *Review of Economic Studies, 33*(4), 309–19.

Kaldor, N. (1967). *Strategic Factors in Economic Development*. Ithaca, NY: New York State School of Industrial and Labor Relations, Cornell University.

Kaldor, N. (1968). Productivity and Growth in Manufacturing Industry: A Reply. *Economica New Series, 35(140)*, 385–91.

Kaldor, N. (1978 [1966]). *Causes of the Slow Rate of Economic Growth of the United Kingdom*. Cambridge: Cambridge University Press.

Kalecki, M. (1954). *Theory of Economics Dynamics: An Essay on Cyclical and Long-run Changes in Capitalist Economy*. London: George Allen and Unwin.

Kanbur, R. (2017). 'Structural Transformation and Income Distribution: Kuznets and Beyond', ESRC GPID Working Paper. London: KCL.

Kaplinsky, R. (2000). Globalisation and Unequalisation: What Can Be Learned from Value Chain Analysis? *Journal of Development Studies, 37*(2), 117–46.

Kaplinsky, R. (2014). Spreading the Gains from Globalization: What Can Be Learned from Value-Chain Analysis? *Problems of Economic Transition*, *47*(2), 74–115.

Kaplinsky, R., & Morris, M. (2016). Thinning and Thickening: Productive Sector Policies in the Era of Global Value Chains. *The European Journal of Development Research*, *28*(4), 625–45.

Karabarbounis, L., & Neiman, B. (2014). The Global Decline of the Labor Share. *The Quarterly Journal of Economics*, *129*(1), 61–103.

Katz, L. F., & Autor, D. H. (1999). Changes in the Wage Structure and Earnings Inequality. In: O. Ashenfelter & D. Card (eds), *Handbook of Labor Economics, Vol 3A*, pp. 1463–555. Amsterdam: Elsevier.

Keynes, J. M. (1939). Relative Movements of Real Wages and Output. *Economic Journal*, *49*(193), 34–51.

Kim, K., & Sumner, A. (2019). The Five Varieties of Industrialisation: A New Typology of Diverse Empirical Experience in the Developing World. *ESRC GPID Research Network Working Paper 18*. London: ESRC Global Poverty & Inequality Dynamics (GPID) Research Network.

Kim, K., & Sumner, A. (2020). De-industrialization, Re-industrialization, and the Resurgence of State Capitalism: The Case of Indonesia. *UNU-WIDER Working Paper 87/2019*. Helsinki: United Nations University—World Institute for Development Economics Research.

Knorringa, P. (2014). Private Governance and Social Legitimacy in Production. In: A. Payne & N. Phillips (eds), *Handbook of the International Political Economy of Governance*, pp. 361–78. Cheltenham: Edward Elgar.

Koopman, R., Wang, Z., & Wei, S.-J. (2014). Tracing Value-Added and Double Counting in Gross Exports. *American Economic Review*, *104*(2), 459–94.

Kowalski, P., Gonzalez, J. L., Ragoussis, A., & Ugarte, C. (2015). Participation of Developing Countries in Global Value Chains: Implications for Trade and Trade-Related Policies. *OECD Trade Policy Papers 179*. Paris: Organization for Economic Cooperation and Development.

Kraay, A. (2006). When Is Growth Pro-Poor? Evidence from a Panel of Countries. *Journal of Development Economics*, *80*(1), 198–227.

Kucera, D., & Milberg, W. (2003). Deindustrialization and Changes in Manufacturing Trade: Factor Content Calculations for 1978–1995. *Review of World Economics*, *139*(4), 601–24.

Kummritz, V., Taglioni, D., & Winkler, D. (2017). Economic Upgrading through Global Value Chain Participation: Which Policies Increase the Value Added Gains? *Policy Research Working Paper No. 8*. Washington, DC: World Bank.

Kunst, D. (2019). Premature Deindustrialization through the Lens of Occupations: Which Jobs, Why, and Where? *Tinbergen Institute Discussion Paper 2019-033/V*. Amsterdam: Tinbergen Institute.

Kuznets, S. (1955). Economic Growth and Income Inequality. *The American Economic Review*, *45*(1), 1–28.

Kuznets, S. (1965). *Economic Growth and Structure, Selected Essays*. New York City, NY: W. W. Norton.

Lakner, C., & Milanović, B. (2015). Global Income Distribution: From the Fall of the Berlin Wall to the Great Recession. *The World Bank Economic Review*, *30*(2), 203–32.

Lewis, W. A. (1954). Economic Development with Unlimited Supplies of Labour. *The Manchester School*, *22*(2), 139–91.

Lewis, W. A. (1955). *The Theory of Economic Growth*. Homewood, IL: Richard D. Irwin.

Lewis, W. A. (1958). Employment Policy in an Underdeveloped Area. *Social and Economic Studies*, *7*(3), 42–54.

Lewis, W. A. (1969). *Aspects of Tropical Trade 1883–1965*. Stockholm: Almqvist & Wiksell.

Lewis, W. A. (1972). Reflections on Unlimited Labor. In: L. E. DiMarco (ed.), *International Economics and Development (Essays in Honour of Raúl Prebisch)*, pp. 75–96. New York City, NY: Academic Press.

Lewis, W. A. (1976). Development and Distribution. In: A. Cairncross & M. Puri (eds), *Employment, Income Distribution and Development Strategy: Essays in Honour of Hans Singer*, pp. 26–42. London: Macmillan.

Lewis, W. A. (1979). The Dual Economy Revisited. *The Manchester School, 47*(3), 211–99.

Lewis, W. A. (2015). *The Evolution of the International Economic Order*. Princeton, NJ: Princeton University Press.

Linden, G., Kraemer, K. L., & Dedrick, J. (2009). Who Captures Value in a Global Innovation Network? The Case of Apple's iPod. *Communications of the ACM, 52*(3), 140–4.

Lindert, P. H., & Williamson, J. G. (2001). Does Globalization Make the World More Unequal? *NBER Working Paper 8228*. Cambridge, MA: National Bureau of Economic Research.

Linkon, S. L. (2018). *The Half-Life of Deindustrialization: Working-Class Writing about Economic Restructuring*. Ann Arbor: University of Michigan Press.

López, M. H. (2017). Trade Liberalization and Premature Deindustrialization in Colombia. *Journal of Economic Structures, 6*(1), 1–30.

López-Calva, L. F., & Ortiz-Juarez, E. (2014). A Vulnerability Approach to the Definition of the Middle Class. *The Journal of Economic Inequality, 12*, 23–47.

Los, B., Timmer, M. P., & deVries, G. J. (2016). Tracing Value-Added and Double Counting in Gross Exports: Comment. *American Economic Review, 106*, 1958–66.

Loungani, P., Saurabh, M., Papageorgiou, C., & Wang, K. (2017). World Trade in Services: Evidence from A New Dataset. IMF Working Paper, WP/17/77. IMF: Washington, DC.

Lustig, N. (2017). Fiscal Policy, Income Redistribution and Poverty Reduction in Low and Middle Income Countries, CEQ Working Paper 54. CEQ Institute, Tulane University.

Maloney, W. F., & Molina, C. (2016). Are Automation and Trade Polarizing Developing Country Labor Markets, Too? *Policy Research Working Paper No. 7922*. Washington, DC: World Bank.

Manning, C., & Purnagunawan, R. M. (2017). Has Indonesia Passed the Lewis Turning Point and Does It Matter? In: H. Hill & J. Menon (eds), *Managing Globalization in the Asian Century: Essays in Honour of Prema-Chandra Athukorala*, pp. 457–84. Singapore: ISEAS Publishing.

Marconi, N., deBorja Reis, C. F., & de Araújo, E. C. (2016). Manufacturing and Economic Development: The Actuality of Kaldor's First and Second Laws. *Structural Change and Economic Dynamics, 37*, 75–89.

Maxwell, S. (2006). What's Next in International Development? Perspectives from the 20% Club and the 0.2% Club. *ODI Working Paper 270*. London: Overseas Development Institute.

McGrath, S. (2018). Dis/articulations and the Interrogation of Development in GPN Research. *Progress in Human Geography, 42*(4), 509–28.

McMillan, M. S., & Rodrik, D. (2011). Globalization, Structural Change and Productivity Growth. *NBER Working Paper No. 17143*. Cambridge, MA: National Bureau of Economic Research.

McMillan, M., Rodrik, D., & Verduzco-Gallo, I. (2014). Globalization, Structural Change, and Productivity Growth, with an Update on Africa. *World Development, 63*, 11–32.

Mensah, E., Owusu, S., Foster-McGregor, N., & Szirmai, A. (2018). Structural Change, Productivity Growth and Labour Market Turbulence in Africa. *UNU-MERIT Working Paper No. 2018–025*. Maastricht: United Nations University—Economic and Social Research Institute on Innovation and Technology.

Milanović, B. (2016). *Global Inequality: A New Approach for the Age of Globalization*. Cambridge, MA: Harvard University Press.

Milberg, W., & Winkler, D. (2011). Economic and Social Upgrading in Global Production Networks: Problems of Theory and Measurement. *International Labour Review, 150*(3–4), 341–65.

Minami, R. (1973). *The Turning Point in Economic Development: Japan's Experience*. Tokyo: Kinokuniya Bookstore Co.

Morrison, A., Pietrobelli, C., & Rabellotti, R. (2008). Global Value Chains and Technological Capabilities: A Framework to Study Learning and Innovation in Developing Countries. *Oxford Development Studies*, 36(1), 39–58.

Mosley, L. (2017). Workers' Rights in Global Value Chains: Possibilities for Protection and for Peril. *New Political Economy*, 22(2), 153–68.

Mudambi, R. (2008). Location, Control and Innovation in Knowledge-Intensive Industries. *Journal of Economic Geography*, 8(5), 699–725.

Musacchio, A., & Lazzarini, S. G. (2014). *Reinventing State Capitalism: Leviathan in Business, Brazil and Beyond.* Cambridge, MA: Harvard University Press.

Myrdal, G. (1956). *An International Economy, Problems and Prospects.* New York City, NY: Harper & Brothers.

Myrdal, G. (1957a). *Rich Lands and Poor: The Road to World Prosperity.* New York City, NY: Harper & Row.

Myrdal, G. (1957b). *Economic Theory and Underdeveloped Regions.* London: Gerald Duckworth & Co. Ltd.

Myrdal, G. (1968). *Asian Drama: An Inquiry into the Poverty of Nations.* New York City, NY: Pantheon.

Myrdal, G. (1970). *The Challenge of World Poverty.* New York City, NY: Penguin Press.

Nayyar, G., Vargas Da Cruz, M. J., & Zhu, L. (2018). Does Premature Deindustrialization Matter? The Role of Manufacturing versus Services in Development. *Policy Research Working Paper, No. 8596.* Washington, DC: World Bank.

Nazeer, N., & Rasiah, R. (2016). Explaining Pakistan's Premature Deindustrialization. *The Lahore Journal of Economics*, 21, 351–68.

Neely, A., Benedetinni, O., & Visnjic, I. (2011).*The Servitization of Manufacturing: Further Evidence.* Paper presented at the 18th European Operations Management Association Conference, Cambridge, July.

Niño-Zarazúa, M., Roope, L. S., & Tarp, F. (2014). Global Interpersonal Inequality: Trends and Measurement. *UNU-WIDER Working Paper Series 2014/004.* Helsinki: United Nations University—World Institute for Development Economics Research.

Nurkse, R. (1953). *Problems of Capital Formation in Underdeveloped Countries.* Oxford: Basil Blackwell.

OECD (2018). *Trade in Value Added Database 2018.* Paris: Organisation for Economic Co-operation and Development.

Oishi, Y., & Paul, S. (2018). Globalization, Structural Transformation, and the Labor Income Share. *ADBI Working Paper No. 893.* Tokyo: Asian Development Bank Institute.

Ortiz-Juarez, E., & Sumner, A. (2021). *Global Income Inequality: An Overview.* London: King's College London.

Oyvat, C. (2016). Agrarian Structures, Urbanization, and Inequality. *World Development*, 83, 207–30.

Page, J. (2012). Can Africa Industrialise? *Journal of African Economies*, 21(2), ii86–ii124.

Pahl, S., & Timmer, M. P. (2019). Patterns of Vertical Specialisation in Trade: Long-run Evidence for 91 Countries. *Review of World Economics*, 155, 459–86.

Pahl, S., & Timmer, M. P. (2020). Do Global Value Chains Enhance Economic Upgrading? A Long View. *The Journal of Development Studies*, 56(9), 1683–1705.

Palma, J. G. (2005). Four Sources of 'De-Industrialisation' and a New Concept of the 'Dutch Disease'. In: J. A. Ocampo (ed.), *Beyond Reforms: Structural Dynamics and Macroeconomic Vulnerability.* Palo Alto, CA: Stanford University Press, 71–116.

Palma, J. G. (2008). De-Industrialization, 'Premature' De-Industrialization and the Dutch Disease. In: S. N. Durlauf (ed.), *The New Palgrave Dictionary of Economics: Volume 1–8*, pp. 1297–1306. London: Palgrave Macmillan.

Pandian, R. K. (2017). Does Manufacturing Matter for Economic Growth in the Era of Globalization? *Social Forces*, 95(3), 909–40.

Patel, D., Sandefur, J., & Subramanian, A. (2018, 15 October). Everything You Know about Cross-Country Convergence Is (Now) Wrong. *PIIE Realtime Economic Issues Watch.*

Phelps, N. A., Atienza, M., & Arias, M. (2018). An Invitation to the Dark Side of Economic Geography. *Environment and Planning A: Economy and Space, 50*(1), 236–44.

Phillips, N. (2017). Power and Inequality in the Global Political Economy. *International Affairs, 93*(2), 429–44.

Pieper, U. (2000). Deindustrialisation and the Social and Economic Sustainability Nexus in Developing Countries: Cross-country Evidence on Productivity and Employment. *The Journal of Development Studies, 36*(4), 66–99.

Pietrobelli, C., & Rabellotti, R. (2011). Global Value Chains Meet Innovation Systems: Are There Learning Opportunities for Developing Countries? *World Development, 39*(7), 1261–9.

Piketty, T. (2014). *Capital in the Twenty-First Century.* Cambridge, MA: The Belknap Press of Harvard University Press.

Piketty, T., & Zucman, G. (2014). Capital Is Back: Wealth-Income Ratios in Rich Countries 1700–2010. *The Quarterly Journal of Economics, 129*(3), 1255–1310.

Piva, M., Santarelli, E., & Vivarelli, M. (2005). The Skill Bias Effect of Technological and Organisational Change: Evidence and Policy Implications. *Research Policy, 34*(2), 141–57.

Polanyi, K. (1957). The Economy as Instituted Process. In: Polanyi, K., Arensberg, C. M., & Pearson, H. W. (eds), *Trade and Market in the Early Empires: Economies in History and Theory*, pp. 243–70. Glencoe: Free Press.

Posthuma, A., & Rossi, A. (2017). Coordinated Governance in Global Value Chains: Supranational Dynamics and the Role of the International Labour Organization. *New Political Economy, 22*(2), 186–202.

Prebisch, R. (1950). *The Economic Development of Latin America and Its Principal Problems.* New York City, NY: Economic Commission for Latin America; also published in *Economic Bulletin for Latin America, 7*, 1–22.

Quah, D. (1996). Twin Peaks: Growth and Convergence in Models of Distribution Dynamics. *Economic Journal, 106*(437), 1045–55.

Ranis, G. (2004). Arthur Lewis' Contribution to Development Thinking and Policy. *Economic Growth Center Yale University Discussion Paper 891.* New Haven, CT: Economic Growth Center Yale University.

Rasiah, R. (2011). Is Malaysia Facing Negative Deindustrialization? *Pacific Affairs, 84*(4), 715–36.

Reddy, S. G., & Lahoti, R. (2015). $1.90 Per Day: What Does it Say? *Discussion Paper No. 189.* Göttingen: Courant Research Centre Poverty, Equity and Growth.

Reijnders, L. S. M., & de Vries, G. J. (2018). Trade, Technology and the Rise of Non- Routine Jobs. *Journal of Development Economics 135*, 412–32.

Rodrik, D. (2013). Unconditional Convergence in Manufacturing. *The Quarterly Journal of Economics, 128*, 165–204.

Rodrik, D. (2016). Premature Deindustrialization. *Journal of Economic Growth, 21*(1), 1–33.

Rodrik, D. (2018). New Technologies, Global Value Chains, and Developing Economies. *Pathways for Prosperity Commission Background Paper Series, No. 1.* Oxford: Pathways for Prosperity Commission.

Rosenstein-Rodan, P. (1943). Problems of Industrialisation in Eastern and Southeastern Europe. *The Economic Journal, 53*, 202–11.

Rosenzweig, M. (1988). Labor Markets in Low Income Countries. In: H. Chenery & T. N. Srinivasan (eds), *Handbook of Development Economics, Volume 1.* Amsterdam: North Holland Press.

Rowthorn, R. E., & Coutts, K. (2004). De-Industrialisation and the Balance of Payments in Advanced Economies. *Cambridge Journal of Economics, 28*(5), 767–90.

Rowthorn, R. E., & Ramaswamy, R. (1997). *Deindustrialization: Its Causes and Implications* (Vol. 10). Washington, DC: International Monetary Fund.

Rowthorn, R. E., & Wells, J. R. (1987). *De-Industrialization and Foreign Trade*. Cambridge: Cambridge University Press.

Saeger, S. S. (1997). Globalization and Deindustrialization: Myth and Reality in the OECD. *Review of World Economics*, *133*(4), 579–608.

Schlogl, L., & Sumner, A. (2020). *Disrupted Development and the Future of Inequality in the Age of Automation*. London: Palgrave Macmillan.

Schultz, T. W. (1964). *Transforming Traditional Agriculture*. New Haven, CT: Yale University Press.

Schumpeter, J. A. (1942). *Capitalism, Socialism and Democracy*. Floyd, VA: Impact Books.

Seers, D. (1963). The Limitations of the Special Case. *Bulletin of the Oxford Institute of Economics and* Statistics, *25*(2), 77–98.

Selwyn, B. (2011). Trotsky, Gerschenkron and the Political Economy of Late Capitalist Development. *Economy and Society*, *40*(3), 421–50.

Selwyn, B. (2012). Beyond Firm-Centrism: Re-integrating Labour and Capitalism into Global Commodity Chain Analysis. *Journal of Economic Geography*, *12*, 205–26.

Shaffer, P. (2019). Introduction. In: P. Shaffer, R. Kanbur, & R. Sandbrook (eds), *Immiserizing Growth: When Growth Fails the Poor*. Oxford: Oxford University Press.

Shaffer, P., Kanbur, R., & Sandbrook, R. (2019). *Immiserizing Growth: When Growth Fails the Poor*. Oxford: Oxford University Press.

Shih, S. (1996). *Me-Too Is Not My Style: Challenge Difficulties, Break Through Bottlenecks, Create Values*. Taipei: The Acer Foundation.

Shin, N., Kraemer, K. L., & Dedrick, J. (2012). Value Capture in the Global Electronics Industry: Empirical Evidence for the 'Smiling Curve' Concept. *Industry and Innovation*, *19*(2), 89–107.

Singh, A. (1977). UK Industry and the World Economy: A Case of De-Industrialization? In: A. Jacquemin & H. W. de Jong (eds), *Welfare Aspects of Industrial Markets. Nijenrode Studies in Economics*, Vol. 2, pp. 183–214. Boston, MA: Springer.

Singh, A. (1987). Manufacturing and De-Industrialization. In: Palgrave Macmillan (eds), *The New Palgrave Dictionary of Economics*. London: Palgrave Macmillan.

Solow, R. M. (1956). A Contribution to the Theory of Economic Growth. *The Quarterly Journal of Economics*, *70*(1), 65–94.

Spitz-Oener, A. (2006). Technical Change, Job Tasks, and Rising Educational Demands: Looking Outside the Wage Structure. *Journal of Labor Economics*, *24*(2), 235–70.

Standing, G. (2011). *The Precariat: The New Dangerous Class*. London: Bloomsbury Publishing.

Stockhammer, E. (2017). Determinants of the Wage Share: A Panel Analysis of Advanced and Developing Economies. *British Journal of Industrial Relations*, *55*(1), 3–33.

Storm, S. (2015). Structural Change. *Development and Change*, *46*(4), 666–99.

Sumner, A. (2010). Global Poverty and the New Bottom Billion: What if Three-Quarters of the World's Poor Live in Middle-Income Countries? *IDS Working Papers*, *2010*(349), 1–43.

Sumner, A. (2012). Where Do the Poor Live? *World Development*, *40*(5), 865–77.

Sumner, A. (2016). *Global Poverty: Deprivation, Distribution, and Development Since the Cold War*. Oxford: Oxford University Press.

Sumner, A. (2018). *Development and Distribution: Structural Change in South East Asia*. Oxford: Oxford University Press.

Sumner, A. (2019). Global Poverty and Inequality: Change and Continuity in Late Development. *Development and Change*, *50*(2), 410–25.

Sumner, A. (2021). *Structural Transformation in Developing Countries*. London: King's College London.

Sumner, A., Yusuf, A. A., & Suara, Y. I. (2014). The Prospects of the Poor: A Set of Poverty Measures Based on the Probability of Remaining Poor (or Not) in Indonesia. *Working Paper in Economics and Development Studies (WoPEDS) 201410*. Bandung: Department of Economics, Padjadjaran University.

Sunkel, O. (1963). El fracaso de las políticas de estabilización en el contexto del proceso de desarrollo latinoamericano. *El trimestre económico, 30*(120(4)), 620–40.

Sunkel, O. (1966). The Structural Background of Development Problems in Latin America. *Weltwirtschaftliches Archiv, 97*(1), 22.

Sunkel, O. (1972). Big Business and 'Dependencia'. *Foreign Affairs, 50*(3), 517–31.

Sunkel, O. (1989). Structuralism, Dependency and Institutionalism: An Exploration of Common Ground and Disparities. *Journal of Economic Issues, 23*(2), 519–33.

Sunkel, O. (1993). *Development from Within: Toward a Neostructuralist Approach for Latin America*. Boulder, CO: Lynne Rienner Publishing.

Sutirtha, R., Kessler, M., & Subramanian, A. (2016). Glimpsing the End of Economic History? Unconditional Convergence and the Missing Middle Income Trap. *CGD Working Paper 438*. Washington, DC: Center for Global Development.

Suzuki, K., Oishi, Y., & Paul, S. (2018). Globalization, Structural Transformation, and the Labor Income Share. *ADBI Working Paper No. 893*. Tokyo: Asian Development Bank Institute.

Syrquin, M. (1988). Patterns of Structural Change. *Handbook of Development Economics, 1*, 203–73.

Szirmai, A. (2012). Industrialisation as an Engine of Growth in Developing Countries, 1950–2005. *Structural Change and Economic Dynamics, 23*(4), 406–20.

Szirmai, A., & Verspagen, B. (2011). Manufacturing and Economic Growth in Developing Countries, 1950–2005. *UNU-MERIT Working Paper No. 2011–069*. Maastricht: United Nations University—Economic and Social Research Institute on Innovation and Technology.

Szirmai, A., & Verspagen, B. (2015). Manufacturing and Economic Growth in Developing Countries, 1950–2005. *Structural Change and Economic Dynamics, 34*, 46–59.

Tan, J. (2014). Running Out of Steam? Manufacturing in Malaysia. *Cambridge Journal of Economics, 38*(1), 153–80.

Tezanos, S., & Sumner, A. (2016). Is the 'Developing World' Changing? A Dynamic and Multidimensional Taxonomy of Developing Countries. *The European Journal of Development Research, 28*(5), 847–74.

Thirlwall, A. P. (1982). Deindustrialization in the United Kingdom. *Lloyd's Bank Review, 144*, 22–37.

Timmer, M. P., & de Vries, G. J. (2009). Structural Change and Growth Accelerations in Asia and Latin America: A New Sectoral Data Set. *Cliometrica, 3*(2), 165–90.

Timmer, M. P., de Vries, G. J., & de Vries, K. (2015). Patterns of Structural Change in Developing Countries. In: J. Weiss & M. Tribe (eds), *Routledge Handbook of Industry and Development*, pp. 65–83. London: Routledge.

Timmer, M. P., Erumban, A. A., Los, B., Stehrer, R., & de Vries, G. J. (2014). Slicing Up Global Value Chains. *Journal of Economic Perspectives, 28*(2), 99–118.

Todaro, M. P. (1969). A Model of Labor Migration and Urban Unemployment in Less Developed Countries. *The American Economic Review, 59*, 138–48.

Tregenna, F. (2009). Characterising Deindustrialisation. *Cambridge Journal of Economics, 33*(3), 433–66.

Tregenna, F. (2014). A New Theoretical Analysis of Deindustrialization. *Cambridge Journal of Economics, 38*(6), 1373–90.

UNCTAD. (2003). *Trade and Development Report 2003. Capital Accumulation, Growth and Structural Change*. Geneva: United Nations Conference on Trade and Development.

UNCTAD. (2013). *Global Value Chains and Development. Investment and Value Added Trade in the Global Economy.* Geneva: United Nations Conference on Trade and Development.

UNIDO (2010). *Industrial Statistics: Guidelines and Methodology.* Vienna: United Nations Industrial Development Organization.

UNIDO (2018). *Global Value Chains and Industrial Development. Lessons from China, South-East and South Asia.* Vienna: United Nations Industrial Development Organization.

UNIDO (2019). *INDSTAT 2 2018.* Vienna: United Nations Industrial Development Organization.

UNSD (2018). *National Accounts Main Aggregates Database.* New York City, NY: United Nations Statistics Division.

UNIDO (2020). *Classification of Manufacturing Sectors by Technological Intensity (ISIC Revision 4).* Vienna: UNIDO. https://stat.unido.org/content/learning-center/classification-of-manufacturing-sectors-by-technological-intensity-%28isic-revision-4%29.

UNU-WIDER (forthcoming). *WIID—World Income Inequality Database.* Helsinki: United Nations University World Institute for Development Economics Research.

Vandermerwe, S., & Rada, J. (1988). Servitization of Business: Adding Value by Adding Services. *European Management Journal,* 6(4), 314–24.

Verdoorn, P. J. (1949). Fattori che Regolano lo Sviluppo Delia Produttivita del Lavoro. *L'Industria.* [Translated in: Thirlwall, A. P. (1988). Population Growth and Economic Development. In: D. Ironmonger, J. Perkins, & T. Hoa (eds), *National Income and Economic Progress: Essays in Honour of Colin Clark.* London: Palgrave Macmillan.]

Wade, R. (1990). *Governing the Market: Economic Theory and the Role of Government in East Asian Industrialization.* Princeton, NJ: Princeton University Press.

Wade, R. H. (2011). Return of Industrial Policy? *International Review of Applied Economics,* 26(2), 223–39.

Wade, R. H. (2014). Market versus State or Market with State: How to Impart Directional Thrust. *Development and Change,* 45(4), 777–98.

Wade, R. H. (2018). The Developmental State: Dead or Alive? *Development and Change,* 49(2), 518–46.

Wallerstein, I. (1979). *The Capitalist World-Economy.* Cambridge: Cambridge University Press.

Werner, M. (2016). Global Production Networks and Uneven Development: Exploring Geographies of Devaluation, Disinvestment, and Exclusion. *Geography Compass,* 10(11), 457–69.

Werner, M. (2018). Geographies of Production I: Global Production and Uneven Development. *Progress in Human Geography.* 43(5), 948–958.

World Bank (2017). *Trouble in the Making? The Future of Manufacturing-Led Development.* Washington, DC: World Bank.

World Bank (2019a). PovcalNet. Washington, DC: World Bank.

World Bank (2019b). *World Development Report 2020: Trading for Development in the Age of Global Value Chains.* Draft Report. Washington, DC: World Bank.

World Bank (2020). *World Development Indicators.* Washington, DC: World Bank.

Wren, A. (ed.). (2013). *The Political Economy of the Service Transition.* Oxford: Oxford University Press.

Ye, M., Meng, B., & Wei, S. J. (2015). *Measuring Smile Curves in Global Value Chains.* Chiba: Institute of Developing Economies, Japan External Trade Organization.

Yeung, H. W.-C. (2015). Regional Development in the Global Economy: A Dynamic Perspective of Strategic Coupling in Global Production Networks. *Regional Science Policy & Practice,* 7(1), 1–23.

Yeung, H. W.-C. (2016). *Strategic Coupling: East Asian Industrial Transformation in the New Global Economy.* Ithaca, NY: Cornell University Press.

Index